ROCK AND ROLL
ECONOMICS

Rock and Roll Economics

Michael Solomon

iUniverse, Inc.
New York Lincoln Shanghai

Rock and Roll Economics

iUniverse, Inc.

For information address:
iUniverse, Inc.
2021 Pine Lake Road, Suite 100
Lincoln, NE 68512
www.iuniverse.com

ISBN: 0-595-28921-5

Printed in the United States of America

Contents

1
Prologue

Many people live for today, but maybe the correct focus is to live for tomorrow. That does not mean that one should be a dreamer. It is that one should focus on tomorrow because today is only the day that tomorrow was yesterday. Therefore to ensure that today will be great, we must take care of tomorrow.

At the current time it seems as if the world has entered a state of "*Virtual Insanity*"[1] and although it cannot be claimed that this work is the answer to all the ills in the world, it has been humbly submitted by its author in an attempt to rationalize the madness and hopefully give the reader a better understanding of the world in which we live and to make the reader better able to negotiate his or her way around the maze of modern life.

This work was written in order to make a contribution to a body of knowledge that has a profound effect over the lives and livelihoods of billions of people around the globe. Management is a privilege and not a right. Along with that privilege goes the responsibility to not abuse subordinates, customers and the other stakeholders who are part of the support structure for the business organization.

---

1.   "*Virtual Insanity*", Jamiroquai, 1997

The Ten Commandments of Rock and Roll Economics

- Be Yourself
- Have It All
- Throw The TV Out The Window
- Smile, You're On Candid Camera
- Give Them Something To Talk About
- Rehearse, Rehearse, Rehearse
- Let Them Come To You
- Keep It Real
- Don't Be A Player-Hater
- Applaud The Losers

2

It's Chaos Man

The black man with the back-to-front cap held centre stage. "Are you ready?" he asked. "Are you ready?" he asked again with even greater urgency. The crowd did not need warming up. They were already excited. The lady pensioners to the left were *extremely* excited. They were waving their pink cowboy hats above their heads with all the energy that they could muster. A few brave women in their company even attempted to blow on the whistles that they had hanging around their necks. The wheelchair-bound pensioners, maybe for the first time, had a chance to thank the disability that had allowed them to obtain a front row seat. "Are you ready?" The voices were getting louder. The middle-aged women in the centre of the auditorium were screaming now. The younger girls were out of their seats unable to contain their exuberance. Women of all ages and sizes were whipping themselves into a frenzy. The warm-up man realized that he was unnecessary and skipped backwards to take his place alongside the two female Afro-Caribbean backing singers. The screens to the left and to the right of the stage displayed an image of the earth from an orbiting satellite. The satellite zoomed in as if carrying an out of the world being towards the earth. The audience erupted as they caught a glimpse of the star of the show. He appeared from the back of the stage. A man of indeterminate age. A goatee beard, slightly hirsute. Afro hair, navy blue suit. A twinkle in his eye—that he could not hide. A bulge in his trousers, at the top his thigh. The warm-up man boomed as the audience went ballistic. "Are you ready, for Mr Tom Jones?" Let us look at the scene again. The dark olive complexion, the melodious voice. The Afro hairstyle. The black bass player. The black drummer. The three black backing singers. The star of the show had come to town to entertain three generations of adoring female fans. He would proceed to tease and gyrate, using his physical presence to thrill the crowd and send them into fits of orgasmic ecstasy. If Tom Jones is *not* a black man then I'm a monkey's uncle.

We will come back to Tom Jones later on. That he is an example of the complexity of the modern world will become quite clear during the course of this brief chapter. His place at the heart of 'rock and roll economics' will reveal itself in time but for now we must familiarize ourselves with the history and importance of 'chaos theory.'

The advent of 'chaos theory' in physics and mathematics has been well documented in scientific circles, but what is not widely recognised is that the research that went into the discovery of what is now known as 'chaos' or 'complexity' theory had its roots in economics just as much as it had its roots in physics. In the 1970s and 1980s, economic forecasting was based on computer systems similar to those used to model weather systems and produce long-term forecasts. Unfortunately, along with the inability to accurately predict the weather over a period of more than a few days, the ability of even the most sophisticated computer systems to accurately predict the economy was sadly lacking. Despite the accuracy and sheer number of input variables, the predictions were erroneous, but the users of the systems clung to their predictions because they so desperately wanted them to succeed. In fact, the governments and financial institutions continued to use them even after the institutions concerned realised that the predictions were next to worthless.[1]

---

1.   *"Chaos"*, p20

The institutions continued to use the computer systems because although the predictions were worthless they still had value even if that value was merely psychological. The human need to predict events, be they climatic or economic, stems from the need to attempt to control the natural environment. The fact that the natural environment is essentially uncontrollable does not deter people from trying to predict the future. Unfortunately this desire often leads to the ascension of people who claim to possess the answer to the prayers of the would-be users of these dubious techniques. It is the sheer number of variables involved in both economic and weather forecasting that makes the pursuit futile. Furthermore, the relationships between the variables are so numerous and complex that small changes in the variables can have repercussions, the extent of which may not be apparent for some time. The result of the use of these computer systems is to give the illusion of control whilst forever playing catch-up with the forces of nature. The physicists who were uncovering 'chaos theory' knew of the use outside of physics and mathematics. They intuitively understood the possible uses in economic forecasting and maybe even in the evolution of society.[2]

It was *because* the physicists knew that their theories were so profound in their chosen fields that they knew the theories must have applications across multiple disciplines. It was *because* the physicists were looking for universal laws that applied across space and time that they looked for patterns where others saw chaos. They looked for order where others saw disorder. They intuitively understood that *because* the forces that controlled the planet had stood the test of time there must be some method in the apparent madness. One only has to think about the reproductive system for a few seconds to begin to unravel the incredible complexity behind the whole essence of human existence. The sheer number of actions and reactions that occur to prompt and facilitate impregnation is quite astounding. There must be order to it, a

---

2.   *"Chaos"*, p20

creative process that must not only apply to humans but also to the majority of the other creatures on the planet. There must be order to it because there are obviously occasions where the order is rearranged. There are instances where some of the actions and reactions work in a *different* way. Not normal, or abnormal, just different. The scientists who were investigating 'chaos theory' knew that the differences were not mere aberrations but were the key to understanding the whole puzzle. To ignore the apparent differences would have been deliberately to walk along the path of ignorance. It is no coincidence that ignorance is derived from the word 'ignore.' It is not possible to ignore a fact and subsequently arrive at the correct answer. The physicists and scientists who worked on 'chaos theory' were determined *not* to be ignorant. They delved into the differences, investigated the exceptions and embedded within the errors they found the correct answer.

The young mathematicians turned a whole branch of mathematics back toward the real world. It was a time of peace, love, and "*experimentation*" in more than one sense of the word. Of course it cannot be claimed that the progress made by the graduate students at Berkeley were as a result of the drug taking prevalent during the 1960s. There is no evidence to support this and it is absolutely reasonable that the decade of "*experimentation*" that led in so many areas to a more holistic view of the world would by-pass the isolated world of mathematics research. By eschewing the distorted view of reality that is a by-product of theoretical simplification in favour of grappling with the complexities of reality, these people were a product of their generation just as much as the NASA scientists who sent man to the dark side of the moon.

As stated previously the investigations into chaos theory in mathematics and physics had its roots in economics. The problem with the economic models at that time was that they did not reflect reality. They magnified and distorted reality whilst claiming that the models were an accurate reflection. It is not really a problem if a mathematical model manages to distort reality. It can still be useful. The fact that some of the output of faulty models can be discarded does not render the whole model valueless. If a model were correct 25% of the time it would still be better than nothing. The problem arises when the creator of the model tries to claim a greater accuracy than is merited by the facts. It is the point at which the model-maker starts to claim that the model is near-100% accurate that it all goes wrong. It can be argued that the 'chaos theory' scientists, in turning their disciplines back toward the real world, have saved society from staring at itself through the fun-house mirror of life.[3]

Robert M. May, one of the leading lights in chaos theory research, claimed that in politics and economics we would all be better off if more people realized that simple systems do not necessarily possess simple dynamics. Although it happens quite frequently in the real world it is still not widely accepted that a supposedly simple system can *include* the behaviour than leads subsequently to complex results. However it is quite obvious in any endeavour that seeks to model the behaviour of humans. The fact that humans are essentially irrational means that even the most predictable outcome can go awry. From mistakes on a production line to 'friendly-fire' in battle situations, human life is full of unintended consequences. It is because of the human element that economic predictions are so often erroneous. In attempting to take a scientific approach to what are deeply psychological decisions, the economists have removed an important element in the economic decision making process. Economists, like biologists, deal with a world of wilful living beings. Unfortunately economists study the most elusive creatures of all.

If genius is the result of the merging of different disciplines into one unique and original idea then Benoit Mandlebrot is a genius. During a

---

3.   A 'fun-house mirror' is the mis-shaped mirror in a circus that distorts the reflection to produce humorous effects.

drawn out career he had tried his hand at economics, mathematics, physics, computing, and a host of other academic disciplines. He was working as a researcher at IBM when he created what became known as the Mandlebrot set.[4] When Mandlebrot was struggling with the presence of 'noise' in transmission errors at IBM, he proposed that engineers should settle for a modest signal, accept the inevitability of errors and use a strategy of 'redundancy' to catch and correct them. The use of the 'redundancy' technique was novel and typical of the attitudes of the chaos scientists. The acceptance of the inevitability of errors rather than persevering with the elimination of errors indicated an acceptance of fate that many of Mandlebrot's peers lacked. The realisation that the errors were predictably random directly led to the discovery of 'chaos theory.'

Mandlebrot claimed that the universe that he was investigating was not smooth and rounded. It was the *"geometry of the pitted, pocked, and broken up, the twisted, tangled, and intertwined."*[5] The oddities in nature are more than mere blemishes; they are often the key to the essence of the thing. It is the geometry of the people, in which the *exception* is the rule and the *error* is the correct answer. The concept of 'colour-blindness', for example, whereby an individual is unable to distinguish between certain colours gives a glimpse into the complexities of reality that is easy to gloss over in the search for scientific truth. The colour red is not necessarily a particular bandwidth of light, as the Newtonians would have it. The concept of redness is a result of human perception. The mathematicians investigating chaos theory were attempting to find formulae to model such universal qualities. The importance of 'chaos theory' can be measured by the fact that it challenges such important scientific facts as Newton's theory of the make up of white light. The fact that an individual is unable to *perceive* cer-

---

4.   The Mandlebrot set is a collection of points in a complex plane. One way to define the set is in terms of a test for every point, involving some simple iterated arithmetic.
5.   *"Chaos"*, p94

tain colours that other people can *perceive* should surely indicate that the colour that is being *perceived* is not in fact real. Once again the *exception* is the rule and the *error* is the correct answer.[6]

The geometry of 'chaos theory' is characterized by the fact that the geometrical boundaries are not discrete but fuzzy. For example, good is taken to mean that which causes pleasure and evil is taken to mean that which causes pain. This is simple enough but unfortunately it is overly simple. There is an aberration that demonstrates the importance of 'chaos theory' in many academic disciplines and across all walks of life. What about an act that causes pleasure to one person and pain to the other? A sadist takes pleasure from causing pain and a masochist takes pleasure from feeling pain. The usual line of enquiry is to ignore these character traits, to treat them as exceptions to the norm and cling to a simplified version of reality. However a 'chaos' line of enquiry leads the observer to recognize that there is *always* pleasure embedded within pain and pain embedded within pleasure. In fact further magnification reveals that the two states are indistinguishable. Therefore if pleasure and pain are indistinguishable it follows that anything that causes pleasure must also cause pain. It therefore follows that good and evil are also indistinguishable. Good will always contain evil, and evil will always contain good. It may be complex, but it is reality.

The discovery of 'chaos theory' was not the product of some grand academic idea or some politician-promoted senate inquiry. There was not even an executive committee of scientists that pushed history into a new direction. It was a product of a few individuals pursuing their own goals. This display of collective individuality is the essence of 'rock and roll economics.' 'Rock and roll economics' is a few like-minded people gathering together with the aim of using their individual talents in a common goal. The more reactionary the goal the more 'rock and roll' it is. If the chaos physicists were 'rock and rollers' then Benoit Mandle-

---

6. *"Chaos"*, p166

brot was the lead singer. Mandlebrot's work at IBM was cutting-edge due to his access to the latest computer technology. One of the most important features of the investigations that led to 'chaos theory' was the concept of 'feedback.' The fact that the new computing power made possible thousands of iterations of the same simple calculation enabled scientific research to take a new experimental path. Of course this dramatic change was taking place against the background of dramatic changes in popular music. The electric guitar had revolutionised popular music. The steel strings, the pickup, and the amplifier had led to the dramatic demonstration of the importance of 'feedback.' With an electric guitar, the pickup recognises the signal from the strings and sends the signal to the amplifier. The amplifier then amplifies this sound and sends it to the loudspeaker. Guitar 'feedback' occurs when the guitar is placed too close to the amplifier so that the sound from the loudspeaker is picked up by the pickup and then transmitted *back* to the amplifier. The amplifier in turn amplifies the amplified sound and it becomes even louder. The result is a sound that quickly intensifies into an unbearable shriek. The dramatic realisation that physicists and mathematicians had come across was that nature was built on such feedback and that the world that we see today is a result of millions and millions of iterations of very simple formulae.[7]

What made the discovery of chaos theory so profound was that it went to the heart of nature and human nature. It sought to explain the natural world and actually succeeded in breaking new ground and overturning preconceived ideas. The phenomenon of 'chaos' is an operational way to define free will, in a way that allows one to reconcile free will with determinism. This is a very important concept because it goes to the heart of human nature. Humans have free will that is also controlled to a large part by a predetermined social and cultural destiny. From housing to education, the choices are pre-determined in that they are dictated to a large extent by financial considerations. However

---

7.   *"Chaos"*, p226

the existence of free will within these constraints is a very crucial factor in the eventual outcome of any individual's life. The unfettered, laissez-faire capitalism that has been allowed to grow unchecked to its ultimate self-destruction is based on the acceptance of the economic superiority of free will without external constraints. On the other hand, the demise of communism demonstrated the economic unacceptability of total pre-determinism with the absence of free will. 'Chaos theory' shows the natural superiority of an economic system that combines free will and pre-determinism. 'Rock and roll economics' is the embodiment of free will within the constraints of a wider society.

'Rock and roll economics' breaks through the problems associated with simplistic models. The problem with any abstract model is always the same. One can make a model more complex and more faithful to reality, or one can make it simpler and easier to handle. The purpose of any model or map is to generalize and abstract. The more accurate the map the more difficult it is to understand and to use. By contrast, the more simple it is, the easier it is to use, but the simplicity comes at the expense of the model failing to reflect reality and probably being worthless. The key to the whole exercise is the use to which the model is to be put. Surely a model, economic or otherwise, needs to be as accurate as possible if it is to be used to aid decisions that affect the lives and livelihoods of millions of people. If this means that an accurate model is too complex to be used then it should be accepted that it is not viable to use abstract models in such cases. There is no law of human nature that says that abstract models need to be used in every decision making process. It must be acceptable that if there is no model that accurately models the weather system, it is not therefore possible to produce accurate long-range weather forecasts. The model makers should of course continue to try to improve their models but if they cannot accurately model reality then surely this is preferable to attempting to change reality in order to protect the vanity of the model makers.

Now that we understand the role that the pioneers of 'chaos theory' have played in the development of human knowledge we can look at the tumultuous changes in the social environment that have laid the foundations for the evolution of 'rock and roll economics.' However before we do that we will illustrate 'chaos theory' at work. To demonstrate the complexity of 'chaos' and to highlight the law of unintended consequence we will now look at the story of 'Mr. B' and 'Mr. C.' 'Mr. C' was the front man for the techno-dance band called The Shamen that was popular in the early 1990s. 'Mr. B' is the son of George Bush senior who was also popular in the early 1990s. It is hard to believe that there may be a link between these two characters, but there is. The answer is in the following items. The first being an extract from George W. Bush's speech launching the *"War on Terror"* in Afghanistan in October 2001, and the second item is an extract from www.solomon-investments.com published a week previously.

Sunday, 7 October, 2001, 18:04 GMT 19:04 UK
Bush opens new front

"The battle is now joined on many fronts. We will not waver. We will not tire. We will not falter and we will not fail."

• President George W. Bush

Source: BBC News

Funds—October 2001 (published 29/09/01 17:59)

"I will not fail nor falter, I shall succeed
My perception is altered, I do believe
Faith is so strong now nothing shall bar my way
Firm conviction, no fiction
This is my day…"

—"Move Any Mountain", *The Shamen*, 1991

Although SIC Global is up 20.0% so far this year SEC regulations dictate that detailed performance figures for the SIC family of funds may only be made available to SIC 'A-list' investors. Please reply with your postal details in order to receive the SIC Global 2002 prospectus.

We hope that everyone remembers that in November 1999 solomon-investments.com said that the stock market could fall by 40%. In March 2000 it didn't seem likely as the Nasdaq headed towards 6000. However at SIC we never wavered from our view and we were ready to *"prophet from it."*

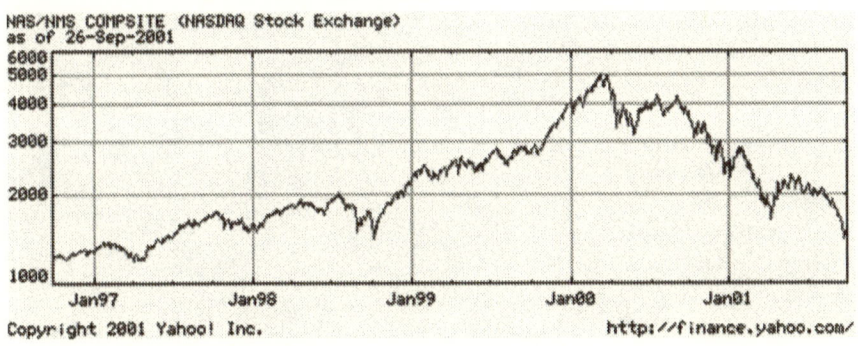

In December 2000 we noted that:

"…the Nasdaq has fallen by almost 50% from its highs, and it would need to rise by 94% from its lows in order to regain those lofty levels.

With hindsight you can see that the March 2000 peak was the perfect selling opportunity. However one could only recognize and act on the selling opportunity if one appreciated that the Nasdaq could fall by 40%.

How much would SIC have saved you if you had acted on the warnings?

Do yourself a favour in 2001. Invest with SIC to ensure that you do not give back the tremendous gains of the last five years."

So now it's October 2001 and all the major averages are heavily in negative territory for the year. So do yourself a favour and invest with solomon-investments.com to ensure that you do not give back the tremendous gains of the last five years!!

Whom else can you trust?

3

We Are Family

It may be stating the obvious, but it seems to have been forgotten over the last few years, that businesses and individuals do not exist in isolation. All organizations and individuals operate within a social and economic environment that either facilitates or hinders the achievement of objectives. Changes within this socio-economic environment, by definition, have a large impact on the success or otherwise of any enterprise. The sociological trends explored in this chapter are diverse, broad, but ultimately connected. Sociologists may tend to group the phenomenon under the catchall heading of 'post-modernism' but the term 'post-modernism' still has no definitive definition and a full description remains as elusive as ever. However for the purpose of 'rock and roll economics' we will use the following description:

> *"A tearing up of the old order and a refusal by individuals to be held hostage to the rigid classifications that had kept previous generations enslaved in the dungeons of their own mind."*

This chapter will examine five areas in which there have been huge changes in the last few decades and examine how the relationships between these changes has made society as a whole much more complex, if not totally chaotic. These five areas are:

- Social attitudes
- The UK class system

- Education
- Women
- Race

It is the combination of the changes in society, mixed with the blurring of the previously rigid class boundaries, flowing into the volcanic changes in the higher education system that have collided and colluded with the massive forces of the post-1960s feminist revolution and the Civil Rights legislations in the United States to create the massive turbulence in the Anglo-American economies.[1] It has taken the breakthrough of 'chaos theory' in physics to explain the forces of turbulence in fluid dynamics and it has taken the breakthrough of 'rock and roll economics' to explain the current turbulence in the Anglo-American capitalist system.

However before we can tackle the complexities of 'rock and roll economics' we must look at the massive forces of change that have been swirling overhead for some time and have only recently come together in such a devastating display of the power and unpredictability of human nature.

Social Attitudes

Planet Earth is the ghetto of the universe. If a ghetto is described as a "*slum area densely populated (especially by one racial group)*" and a slum is defined as "*a mean or dirty street or neighbourhood*" then is it clear that the problems of the world and humanity in general are derived from the fact that the earth is, in universal terms, a ghetto. For instance, in the United States, the ghettoes of New York and Los Angeles are characterized by violence and conflict because of the oppression by the ruling class. This oppression causes self-hatred to

---

1.   The essence of turbulence is that it is an unseen force and exists as a property of the external climate.

manifest itself in the oppressed population. In the same way, forces of nature that are beyond human control continue to rule humans. Humans live with the uncertainty of a certain fate and there is absolutely nothing that can be done about it. This leads humans to hate themselves individually and to hate each other collectively. This one fact leads to the constant wars and general violence in society.

If Earth were a ghetto relative to the rest of the universe then like any other ghetto one would expect to find rats. Unfortunately humans do not like rats. They are viewed as vermin and are destroyed whenever they stray into human encampments. The capitalist corporate world is referred to as a 'rat race' in which every participant wants to be a success. Everybody wants to be well regarded by their family, peers, and the rest of the society but it must be presumed that to be a success in the 'rat race' one has to be the best at whatever it takes to be the *winner* in the 'rat race'. Therefore we must assume that the biggest, toughest, most ruthless rat is the one that wins the 'rat race.' However unfortunately for the winners of the 'rat race', humans do not like rats.

At the present time 'gangs,' 'drug dealers,' and 'criminals' have taken control of the ghetto. There are 'gangs' such as bullying governments that oppress their citizens. There are 'drug dealers' such as the cigarette and alcohol companies that profit from peddling toxic substances to children. There are also the 'criminals' in suits that have stolen trillions of dollars from society unchallenged, aided and abetted by the governments that are supposed to be working on the behalf of society. This need to dominate on the part of certain individuals and organizations is a part of human nature but it has increased in popularity and acceptance as a result of the spread of Nazi ideology before, during, and after the Second World War. The Nazis based their ideals on Nietzsche's rejection of Christianity and the idea that dominance was the true goal of man. However if Jesus Christ actually lived he must have been some person. It is quite an achievement to have some people speak about a man on a daily basis some two thousand years after that man's death. To have people exclaim his name during the heights of passionate love making, and for it not to seem unusual, has to be one of the greatest personal achievements of all time. So the question remains outstanding as to what on earth did this person *actually* do to achieve such long-lasting fame and notoriety? Whatever it was it obviously transcends time and must strike at the heart of what it is to be human. For generation after generation to refer back to this man who died two thousand years ago must mean that there was something about the man that resonates throughout time.[2]

However times have changed and there is a general acceptance that society has become more secular, and that capitalism has become the primary economic and social force in the world. Capitalism as we see it operating today is based on a 'dog eat dog' mentality. Companies have adopted a policy of superiority and dominance over competitors, customers, employees, and in some cases, of dominance over the company's host government.[3] With the decline of religion and its associated icons, there has grown in its place whole industries dedicated to creating new idols for people to worship. The film and music industry, politics, and even business are increasingly being driven by the devotion to celebrities, idols, and demigods. If one looks closely at these people, and they are after all still people, you will see, especially among the women, a preponderance of bleached blonde hair. These people are all seeking to

---

2. Therefore if Jesus Christ actually lived it must follow that the concept of "*Peace and Love*" must be innately human for it to have found such empathy over the centuries.

3. See Microsoft v Justice Department and Vodafone v Inland Revenue.

model themselves along the lines of the Aryan ideal. The blonde hair, blue eyed, young, physically fit specimen. Society in general is being encouraged to aspire to what is in essence the Nazi ideal.

Class

The Anglo-American class system is split horizontally and organized as a hierarchy. However, in reality, the class system is less like a rigid hierarchy and more like a circle. There is not as much difference between the working class and the upper class as one might think. The upper class people are merely people who have *completed* their work. They have been rewarded for it and they do not have anything else to do. However the working class is prevented from rising through society to the upper class by the presence of the middle class. The middle class continuously frustrates the working class and prevents its members from finishing their work.[4] This suits the middle class because they merely aspire to the supervisory roles in society. If the middle class had any ambition they would quickly rise to join the upper class. At the present time the Anglo-American class system has reached an impasse because the working class work but they do not show loyalty, and the middle-class are loyal but they refuse to do any work.

Furthermore, 80% of Americans see themselves as middle class.[5] Unfortunately according to strict definitions, many are in fact working-class. It seems that much of the middle class has been downgraded by stealth to such an extent that it no longer exists. The advances in technology, especially comput-

---

4. Downsizing, outsourcing has removed whole layers of middle managers. The popularity of Michael Porter's 'value-chain' analysis heavily influenced corporations in the 1990s.

5. *"Oxford Dictionary of Politics"*

ing power, have virtually made the middle class redundant. They feel it, and fear it, but they still cling to the notion that they are middle class. In addition, with the expansion of university education in Britain since the mid-1980s, this once proud bastion of middle-class virtue has been thrown open to the working-class. The university system is no longer solely educating the middle-class, it is now providing 'further training' for the working-class. Overall, the downgrading of the middle-class is not perceived as a problem because it is happening quite slowly. However there is a whole generation desperately clinging on to a fast-diminishing past in the face of a stark new reality.

By way of contrast, in 'rock and roll economics' the class system is split vertically. It is split between good and bad to form a continuum along the x-axis. In 'rock and roll economics' it is acknowledged that in any profession, in any walk of life, in any social sphere, there will be some people who do a good job and who are a credit to society. Unfortunately there are those at the other end of the continuum. There are those in society who just *love* to do wrong. In 'rock and roll economics' it is accepted that no social group is exempt from the human condition and part of that human condition is the temptation to do what one knows to be wrong. The split along the x-axis on the class continuum recognizes that there are good dustmen and bad dustmen. There are good capitalists and bad capitalists. Good accountants and bad accountants. It is all quite simple really. Unfortunately the criminal justice system is currently breaking down because it does not acknowledge the existence of criminals. By adopting the philosophy of "*innocent until proven guilty,*" the current system merely recognizes 'crimes' and people accused of 'crimes.' It does not acknowledge that there are some people who just *love* to do wrong.[6]

Education

Cast your mind back to the times when primitive man roamed the landscape and obtained food primarily by hunting. It was a tough time with bandits to contend with in addition to the wild animals. An intelligent person in modern society is like a person with twenty-twenty vision in primitive times. In primitive times the person with perfect vision would have been able to see any dangers that may have lurked in the distance and could warn the tribe in enough time so that preventative action could be taken. A person with myopia, commonly known as shortsightedness, would obviously be at a great disadvantage, and one that may at some point cost the person his life. In this analogy, intelligence is the ability to 'see' and education is that transfer of knowledge between the person with good eyesight and the person with myopia. However this 'education' process only works for the benefit of the myopic person as long as the person with twenty-twenty vision has his best interests at heart. If this is not the case it is quite possible that the view of the landscape that the fully sighted person relays to the myopic person is in fact misleading. The myopic person finds out too late that he has been mislead and is killed. One may think that, *"once bitten twice shy,"* but the key for the evil person with twenty-twenty vision is that of trust. The myopic person must trust the sighted person even though he continues to be misled. He would be better off killing the person with twenty-twenty vision and just taking his chances with the wild animals and the bandits. In modern society the most danger-

6. For example, Dr Harold Shipman was able to murder hundreds of his elderly patients in his small village near Manchester because his death certificates were not checked. No one suspected that this bespectacled doctor was in fact killing his patients and stating that the deaths were natural. The exact number of Dr Shipman's victims will probably never be known.

ous person is the intelligent, evil person whom society continues to trust despite continuously being let down.

The education process in modern society is designed to identify the people who are intelligent enough to figure out the answer for themselves, and to 'educate' them with the *wrong* answer before they have a chance to see the reality for themselves. However the Anglo-American education system is not an education system at all. It is a mis-education system. It is designed to mislead whole swathes of the population. Intelligence is the ability to figure out the answer for oneself, but education is society's way of *giving* people the answer. However that would be fine if the answer that they were given was the *right* answer, but it is not. By creating a hierarchical education system, society weeds out the citizens who are intelligent enough to figure out the answer and 'educates' them with the *wrong* answer before they have a chance to think for themselves. They are given the *wrong* answer but they believe it is the *right* answer and because they are supposedly intelligent, they are no longer in a position to be told that they have got it *wrong*. They then enforce the *wrong* answer on the rest of society until they finally figure it out for themselves. By that time it is usually too late.

This is how it works and how it has always worked, but as the barriers to higher education are being removed it is becoming increasingly difficult for the sons and daughters of the previously oppressed citizens to embrace a philosophy and a way of life that is the *cause* of their plight rather than the *solution* to their plight.

Education is not and should never be about "*getting a degree to get a good job.*" To be employed is tantamount to being a slave no less that when the poor of society were forced to toil in workhouses in order to earn their basic food and shelter.

Therefore a good job is still nothing more than being a well-paid slave. Education is and should always be about freedom. It is about setting the mind of a child free, so that the body may follow. Universities were previously middle-class institutions but with the opening up of the education system there is increasing competition for places. It seems that the acceptance of students from working class backgrounds reflects a change in the attitude that the ruling class have towards universities.[7] They have become in effect institutions for training people for work rather than educating them. In Britain there is now a widening gulf in the perceived level of quality of 'Oxbridge', the other traditional universities, and the newer universities.

Finally, sociologists talk about 'life-chances' as if they are absolutes. They totally disregard the concept of talent. It is probably because talent is defined as *"natural ability"* and the education system seems to dislike this concept intensely. They fear it above all. However the increasing importance of talent in modern society totally transforms the probabilities determined by a person's 'life chances.' In fact, talent allied with hard work increasingly renders the concept almost meaningless because the hard work is increasingly being used to overcome any *artificial* barriers that are placed in a person's path.

Women

The radical feminists do not like the unequal status that 'traditional' female roles carry in society. The declared goal of the radical feminists is to 'de-stratify' society in order to make it

---

7. This is because a privilege assumes a right granted to only a few people. Therefore once everyone has the right, it ceases to be a privilege and no advantage can be gained from possessing it. For example, the UK housing market buoyed by record mortgage lending has become a 25 year debt trap for a whole class of society.

more equal. This strategy entails dragging men *down* to their own level instead of women attempting to *rise* up the hierarchy. Unfortunately not all roles in society carry equal status. This is an important concept. There needs to be an incentive for someone to do the more important and more difficult roles.[8] Not every person *wants* to be a leader. Some people are content to be followers, therefore leaders must lead and followers must follow. To elect to be a follower and then to refuse to follow is tantamount to introducing anarchy. This seems to be what the radical feminists desire. They are currently attempting to destroy the institution of marriage, and it is increasingly becoming something of a sick joke. The current trend in advertising clearly demonstrates this. Images of miserable women who despise their male partners are to be seen used to sell everything from mobile phones to cigarettes.

For Afro-Caribbean people to progress in an Anglo-American society they need to get out of the ghettoes. For women to rise up in a male dominated society they need to get out of the mental ghetto called 'feminism.' Any political movement that seeks to destroy the status quo instead of promoting peaceful integration will instead find itself destroyed by that status quo. The contradiction and the fatal flaw in the feminist position is that women still need the physical protection of men. The deep biological need for protection from a hostile external environment still remains to the present day. This presents a problem because in a physical confrontation with a male, the female will almost certainly come off worse. So now that the campaign for equal rights has metamorphosed into radical feminism, men no longer have an incentive to continue to police the social movement. Therefore the only way that femi-

---

8.   Maslow's hierarchy of needs is important here as is Adam Smith's work on the importance of division of labour to the success of nations.

nism can succeed is through stealth. Stealth has worked up until now but unfortunately the obvious bragging about relative female achievement, e.g. school results, has created a vicious backlash.

Meanwhile at home, the marriage roles remain the same as in the days when humans were hunter-gatherers. During those times, tribes of men roamed the landscape hunting for food to bring back to their families. Now the tribe is the 'company' and the food that is hunted is the 'consumer.' The problem with this situation in the modern world is that the consumer is quite often the wife and family. Furthermore the supply-side reforms of the 1980s have increased the number of 'tribes' that are hunting the consumer. The tribes are literally killing themselves to get the consumer. However, the consumer is getting cleverer and becoming increasingly hard to catch, but the tribes are trying harder and harder. To make matters worse, the tribe members are also consumers—hence the hunters are also the hunted.

It is even more complex when it comes to the family finances. When only men went out to work, a man would bring home an income of £30,000 for example. He would be expected to share this with his wife and children. So for the sake of simplicity let us say the husband and wife split the spoils in half and they both had £15,000 each.[9] These days with women encouraged to work and more and more women, especially young women, taking up the challenge, the working environment has become more competitive. Now if we fast-forward to the logical conclusion of this trend we reach the point where all women work and men still do not stay at home with the children. Because the amount of money in society that may be earned has not increased, because it cannot increase, the man

9.   This is merely a gross simplification to make a point.

and the woman are now competing for the same £30,000 job. Unfortunately the way that the conflict is being resolved is by splitting the job in two. Now the man and the woman are working side-by-side doing half a job each for half the money. In this way the household income remains at £30,000 but they are both working twice as hard for half the money. This is because the act of 'working side by side as a team' merely masks intense internal rivalry. The single woman has more financial freedom than before, but the cost only sinks home when she matures. If she has children and stays at home the household income drops dramatically to £15,000 but the husband is still working twice as hard because another person has filled the woman's job. So now £15,000 is used to support the husband, wife, and the new baby. Financial pressures plus work pressures equal divorce. The radical feminists have won, but at the expense of destroying the whole fabric of society. Once again it is all out war in the 'battle of the sexes' and the radical feminists have trained a whole army of 'economic suicide bombers' who have been unleashed on an unsuspecting world.

Race

Racism will only be wiped out when we all understand that we are all part of one big family. Race itself is a concept that is not borne out by reality. The genes that make up the physical differences between humans are few and far between. We are just one big family of humans living on the same planet. Some of us have dark hair, some of us have blonde hair, and some of us have ginger hair. Some of us have light skin, some of us have brown skin, and some of us have dark skin. Society is increasingly accepting that despite the protestations from a vocal minority, "*it really doesn't matter if you're black or white.*"[10] We are still family. Of course that does not mean that we will get along with all our relatives all of the time. Every family will have disagreements from time to time but the family bond can never be broken. It is quite ridiculous to say that someone with ginger hair is a lesser person than someone with black hair. It is quite foolish to subscribe to a theory that people with brown hair are inherently more intelligent than people with blonde hair.

Furthermore with the increasing racial awareness since the 1960s, there have been attempts to build multi-cultural communities and to foster a multi-cultural society. Unfortunately there is a fatal flaw in this proposition. This is because multiple cultures in a society will always lead to conflict. Culture by definition is a shared set of norms and values. To have a multi-cultured society means to have a society made up of discrete groups with differing norms and values. The groups will always be in conflict unless tolerance is a primary value shared between the groups. However, once important values are shared amongst all the people it ceases to become a multi-cultured society. We are back to a single culture that happens to tolerate difference. That is the goal, but unfortunately Anglo-American society is a million miles away from that goal at the present time. Unfortunately the benefits of promoting difference and racial conflict continue to outweigh the benefits of promoting tolerance and inclusion.

In summary, the result of the swirling changes in the above areas has created a vortex that is causing turbulence in the established order. The old rules that applied to a more structured society have broken down and have become an embarrassing relic of a bygone era. The rules that were previously set in stone have not yet been completely smashed but they are currently being *ignored* and are crumbling away due to a lack

---

10. Extract from "*Black or White*" by Michael Jackson, the only person in human history to change the colour of his skin.

of maintenance. If the Anglo-American capitalist system is to avoid breaking down completely, it needs to quickly embrace 'rock and roll economics.' Therefore it is imperative that we move on to describing 'rock and roll economics' and why it is the only hope to avoiding the whole-scale demolition of the Anglo-American capitalist system that is already underway.

4

Rock And Roll Economics

The concept of 'rock and roll economics' attempts to tackle the management of the complexities in the economic system. 'Rock and roll economics' begins by accepting that economic choices, as in other areas of life, are fraught with difficulties and contradictions. Economic choices are not straightforward choices based upon rational decisions regarding units of 'satisfaction'. Real life is more complex than that, and any economic model that is not based on reality will result in unrealistic predictions and dangerous outcomes.

Complexity in any system, as it is in life, cannot be removed. It is similar in principle to the law of physics that states that momentum passes from object to object. In trying to remove complexity, all that is achieved is moving the complexity from one place to another. For example, many of the theories in the social sciences such as 'social class' in sociology, are based on gross simplifications. The result of these gross simplifications is that the study of complex social and economic interactions is made easier. This simplification also makes it appear easy to predict the outcomes of various social situations and stimuli. Unfortunately this psuedo-scientific knowledge has not removed the complexity. The complexity has merely been passed on to the subjects under observation. The individuals whose actions are supposedly known and predictable are then *forced* to comply with these rules because so many national institutions are founded upon them. If, in order to achieve a satisfactory outcome, the individuals are successful in adapting to these rules then the psuedo-scientists go on to claim further proof for their pet theories. However, if the individuals choose not to comply with these rules they are termed deviant and their chances of progress within society will be limited.[1] The net result of all this activity is that the individuals take on the complexity of the real world in order that the psuedo-scientist academics can continue to live in a fantasy world of certain knowledge in an uncertain world. However some of these individuals cannot tackle the complexity of the 'real world' from within the straightjacket of socio-economic theory, and increasing numbers find themselves falling into the growing band of people that make up the 'underclass' in Western society.

In reality, everyone is an individual who has a unique past, both genetic and cultural, and therefore the desires of individuals are equally unique and difficult to classify. It follows that the correct order of things is for individuals' lives to be straightforward, but the study of these interactions should by necessity be very complex and probably out of the reach of psuedo-scientists. For example, in the United Kingdom there are two main political parties and a third minor party. This means that approximately forty million individuals are required to choose between these three parties or choose not to vote at all. In fact, the number of people electing not to vote is increasing and at some point it will be greater than the number of people who do vote. One would have thought that forty million people would warrant at least one hundred different shades of political party. For instance, 'New Labour Republican Green Euro-sceptic' could be an interesting shade that would represent the views of many people. By way of contrast, another similar but different shade could be 'Old Labour Republican Green Euro-phobe'. However at the current time, membership of a

---

1.   The Oxford Dictionary of Sociology defines deviance as *"a formal property of social situations and social systems."* It is also defined as *"a pattern of norm violation"* whereby an individual is defined as deviant by not adhering to the standard behaviour of society.

political party entails wholesale acceptance of the party line. This is in effect a form of forced agreement that is perpetuated because the illusion of consensus within the political party is the only reason for the party's existence. If the consensus did not exist, voters would have no reason to vote for a particular party because the voters would not be clear on the policies that would be implemented in their name. Democracy is supposed to represent the will of the voters—and so the parties must cling to the illusion of consensus despite the differences of opinion between the party members.

Therefore 'rock and roll economics' states that life is uncertain and that we must accept it as it is. Any attempt to control life by force will ultimately meet with failure. 'Rock and roll economics' is based on the same ideals as rock and roll music. This is because the essence of 'rock and roll economics' is an acceptance of individual freedom, individual choice, and individual dignity. However to understand rock and roll music we must take a brief look back at music history. 'Rock and roll' music is derived from 'blues' music. 'Blues' music was derived from the music sung by slaves in the cotton plantations in the Deep South of the United States. 'Blues' was a way of enhancing life by turning tragic situations into entertainment. It was sad music but, at least initially, not rebellious music. The slave masters permitted the music because it enhanced slave productivity. 'Blues' music evolved into 'rock and roll' and entered the mainstream when it was popularised by white musicians such as Elvis Presley. The attitude that 'rock and roll' reflects and reinforces has survived and thrived. Rock and roll music has evolved into many different genre such as punk in the late 1970s and rap music in the early 1980s. Rock and roll music now has a rebellious edge that 'blues' music lacked. Each one of these disparate genres however is derived from rock and roll so that rock and roll can be used to sum up an attitude, a point of view, and a style. It is first and foremost about individual expression within the confines of a wider society. Rock and roll music celebrates and encourages rebellion. Over the generations the recording industry has grown so that its influence over the minds of citizens, especially teenagers, is so great so as to pose a real threat to any social organization based upon an unswerving acceptance of command and control policies.[2]

In 'rock and roll economics' the society is seen as 'the band'. In rock and roll music the requirements of the band come before the requirements of any individual. The singer is the lead singer for the band, the songwriter is the songwriter for the band, and the manager is the manager for the band and so on. In the same way the fans are fans of the band and the music and merchandise that is consumed is a way of displaying loyalty to the band. The band may change the singer, the songwriter, or the manager but the allegiance that the fans have to the band remains. Even after the band has disbanded there may still be a loyal following who represent a latent demand for more music and merchandise. This is evidenced by the continued popularity of artists such as Elvis Presley and John Lennon whose estates continue to generate huge profits as a result of a loyal fan base. The revenues generated by these estates, over twenty years after the death of the artist, often eclipse the earnings of the major artists of the present day. In a rock and roll band, the band members strive to do what is best for the band above and beyond what is best for the individual band member. The philosophy behind this is of mutual dependence and an acceptance that the prosperity of any band member is intrinsically linked to the prosperity of the band as a unit. This stands in contrast to modern economic theory that states that society is best served by individuals acting out of their own self-interest. In 'rock and roll economics' the individuals in society recognize that their individual needs are best met by doing what is best for society. Rather than merely comparing economic choices one against the other, 'rock and roll economics' reflects the knowledge that

---

2. Eminem was introduced to the world and produced by Dr Dre. Dr Dre was previously a member of the infamous rap group NWA. Eminem is now a triple platinum selling white rap artist who is converting a whole generation of middle-class children to black music. Coincidently, NWA is short for N*****s With Attitude.

these choices are also linked with, and are dependent upon, society as a whole.[3]

'Rock and roll economics' also accepts that excesses will occur but that they should be dealt with in a better way. In 'rock and roll economics' it is better to deal with the *actual* excesses that occur rather than seek to contain them by assuming that a problem *will* occur merely because an economic model states that it will. 'Rock and roll economics' assumes that the individuals who behaved in such a way at such a time in the past as to cause the phenomenon that is the subject of the economic model are thinking human beings who are unlikely to repeat the actions that led to the unfortunate outcome. For example, UK home-buyers are unlikely to over-extend themselves in the same way as they did in the late 1980s housing boom. The individuals who had their homes repossessed, or knew of others who had their homes repossessed would act rationally by modifying their actions in order to avoid a repeat situation. This would be all well and good but how does this explain the emergence of a new boom in the early 2000s? One factor may be the 'buy-to-let' initiative by the Association of Residential Letting Agents (ARLA) and the Council of Mortgage Lenders (CML). The 'buy-to-let' initiative encouraged people to borrow to purchase properties in addition to their main residence. Individuals could then borrow without the threat of repossession of their main residence. In addition, the mortgage lenders would avoid the negative publicity associated with repossessions. Furthermore relatively low interest rates allowed people to borrow a higher multiple of their salaries then they had been able to previously. The concern about the *total* repayment

---

3. 'Rock and roll economics' is also based on the same principles as the 'Theory Y' management style. 'Theory X' and 'Theory Y' are two conflicting theories regarding the human motivation to work, put forward by the US psychologist Douglas McGregor. 'Theory X' is based on the premise that people are inherently lazy, dislike work, and will avoid it if they can. 'Theory Y' on the other hand assumes that people wish to be interested in their work and given the right conditions, will enjoy it. The generally accepted view is that if management follow 'Theory Y' they will achieve better operational performance.

burden was not an issue in the early 2000s as it was in the late 1980s. In the late 1980s some house buyers stretched themselves by buying a house with a large mortgage as a percentage of the purchase price. Unfortunately, when interest rates rose dramatically in the late 1980s, these borrowers found that the repayment burden was too onerous and repossessions rose dramatically. By way of contrast, in the early 2000s, borrowers are confident about being able to meet repayments on a loan of more than three times salary but the mortgage lenders have, by relaxing the rules, allowed property prices to inflate dramatically thereby causing a new UK housing market bubble. Different actions. Different causes. However, the same result. The Bank of England (BoE) has allowed this boom/bust scenario to unfold because of an almost child-like fascination with the possible return of an inflationary wage-price spiral. The BoE's standard economic models have failed to predict the creation of another asset price bubble. In contrast, 'rock and roll economics' embraces the complexities of reality and this enables the model to explain, predict, and finally prevent the economic excesses that lead to boom and bust. If we look at the economy of the mid-1970s we can see 'rock and roll economics' at work.

It was after the rampant inflation of the 1970s that the control of inflation became the primary economic goal in the western economies. Prior to the 1970s, inflation had not really been much of a problem.[4] However, after the 1970s the control of inflation became an obsession within the world's central banks. It was as a result of this inflation shock that economic models such as NAIRU gained in prominence.[5] The idea was promoted that strong growth *automatically* leads to a rise in inflation. There however, is not an *automatic* link because reality is more complex than this. The inflation of the 1970s had many causes that formed the connection between the strong growth in the economy

---

4. *"The Death of Inflation"*
5. NAIRU is the Non-Accelerating Inflation Rate of Unemployment. The theory states that inflation will accelerate if unemployment were to fall below a certain level.

and the inflation that resulted. For instance, the quadrupling of the oil price by the OPEC cartel had nothing to do with the tendency of consumers to loosen their purse strings when it looks like the economic going is good. When a cartel such as OPEC raises the price of a basic commodity so dramatically, the ripple effect is felt throughout the economy. Fortunately enough, one of the major policy changes that resulted from the 1970s inflation shock was a commitment to break the links between strong growth and inflation. Whether it was the power of a cartel such as OPEC, or the power of the trade unions to bring the United Kingdom to a halt by calling for a three-day week, the links between strong growth and inflation had to be broken. This is the point that Margaret Thatcher, Ronald Reagan, and the monetarist economists such as Milton Friedman entered the picture. Rightly or wrongly, these people implemented the policies that finally broke the link between economic prosperity and rampant inflation.

Therefore 'rock and roll economics' explains that the inflation was caused by the rebellion of OPEC and the trade unions against the economic government of the day. The inflation was not caused by the economic choices of the participants in the wider economy. A few individuals expressing themselves in their own way caused the rampant inflation. 'Rock and roll economics' therefore directly challenges the acceptance of rationality that economic theory is based upon. In 'rock and roll economics' it is absolutely rational to behave in an irrational and rebellious way. It is entirely expected that a few individuals will gather together and seek to cause trouble. It is because of this acceptance of reality that 'rock and roll economics' demands that the citizens in the wider economy do not suffer for the actions of a few 'rock and rollers'.

The irrationality of rationality in economics is no better illustrated than by examining the Efficient Market Hypothesis (EMH). Standard economic thinking leads to theories such as EMH that make sense from a purely academic point of view but whose substance melts away when exposed to the glare of common sense and reality. EMH is born out of an acceptance of rationality but it completely ignores human nature and more importantly, it completely ignores common sense. EMH states that financial markets cannot be beaten because everything that can influence the share price is already known. This is true to a large extent but it ignores one crucial fact—the fact that humans are involved and that there is a decision-making process that does not occur in isolation. Therefore before something is decided, people know. As it is being decided, people know. After it has been decided, and before it is reported, people know. As long as there is a financial incentive that outweighs the punishment, people will trade on these whispers and half-facts. In fact if EMH is true it suggests that the only way of beating the market is by insider trading. Therefore EMH by definition proves itself to be false. If EMH is true then only by 'beating expectations' can share prices rise. Unfortunately 'expectations' are increasingly managed by the company in order that the company can exceed them and keep the share price rising. Therefore manipulation of the accounts is not only commonplace but it is the most popular way to run a public business in an environment where the investment tail wags the corporate dog.

Since the arrival of the corporate raiders of the late 1980s,[6] the financial markets have held the power over corporations by promoting management incentives to get share prices rising. However, once share prices had risen above fair value, these incentives corrupted the whole exercise. Investors became addicted to the rising prices and did not care how they were achieved. Early and wise long-term investors bailed out and protested but the new legions of 'day-traders' did not care about academic protestations about an over-valued stock market.[7] The venture capitalists, company executives, brokers, fund managers, and jour-

---

6. *"Takeover"*
7. 'Day traders' are mainly individual traders who trade in and out of stocks on a daily basis with the aim of generating short-term profits.

nalists were 'rocking and rolling' the stock market, but the wider economy was doing very well thank you. The 'day-traders' were making good money riding the boom and they were not worried where the money came from. In their eyes the money was real so who cared. No one cared, that is until it all went berserk in 1999 after the Federal Reserve Chairman Alan Greenspan started to lose his mind.

Alan Greenspan struggled to cope with the economic excesses using standard economic theory, but standard economic theory was found wanting. According to J.K. Galbraith, it is tantamount to economic suicide for a central banker to pump money into the economy only to suddenly withdraw it.[8] That is exactly what Alan Greenspan did in response to the Y2K threat. The banks lent out the money to 'day-traders' who speculated in Nasdaq stocks on margin and when the Federal Reserve called in the money, the stockbrokers pulled in the margin facilities from their clients and the Nasdaq dropped sharply. Once prices start falling the previous speculative cycle was quickly reversed.

If the President of the United States is forced by legislation to leave office after eight years, irrespective of how good a job he has done, why is it that the Federal Reserve chairman can remain in office unchallenged for fifteen years? It is arguable that, in an age where the US Congress and the US Senate are deadlocked, the Federal Reserve has more power than the President. Such power in an un-elected official over such a long period is bound to cause inefficiencies. The crunch for the Federal Reserve came with the Long Term Capital Management (LTCM) disaster in 1998. Alan Greenspan saved his cohorts in LTCM when there was no threat to the economy as a whole. There was no systemic threat because of the basic rule that for every party there is counter-party. It therefore follows that as a bank loses, another bank gains. It is therefore obvious even to the layperson that taking the financial system as a whole, there would be no change and no recovery

---

8.   *"The Great Crash of 1929"*

action would be required. In fact, no action would have been the best response because it would have acted to cure the speculative excesses at the time. Alan Greenspan's actions only served to create the so-called 'Greenspan put' whereby it is assumed that the Federal Reserve will bail out any potential disaster and thereby provide a floor under the market. Greenspan had in fact created a 'moral hazard' in the financial markets that at some point needed to be resolved.[9] Only in 'rock and roll economics' is it acknowledged that the central bankers may be part of the problem. By seeking to control the excesses in the economy it is quite clear that Alan Greenspan became a 'rock and roller' himself.

With the benefit of hindsight it is easy to see that policy errors were made and that the band of people saying "*I told you it was too good to be true*" has grown and grown. However we should not forget that there was a unique point in time that the economy was very, very good and it was all very, very true. Let us remind ourselves how good the good times were.

The following are extracts from www.solomon-investments.com written in March and April 2000.

Roundup (United States)

The GDP growth rate of 7.3% for the fourth quarter of 1999 sounded incredibly fast, but the year on year growth rate was *only* 4.2%. This was in fact lower that the 1998 growth rate of 4.3%.

The Federal Reserve is pretending that the 7.3% growth rate for Q4 1999 was a result of the tight labour market and a "*wealth effect*" resulting from rising real estate and stock prices.

This is absolute nonsense and they know it! The 7.3% growth was a direct result of the liquidity that the Fed pumped into the bank-

---

9.   'Moral Hazard' is the term used for the incentive to cheat in the absence of penalties for cheating. It usually manifests itself in the concealment of information from regulatory bodies and or senior executives.

ing system in order to avert a potential Y2K crisis. The banks then lent this liquidity out to individuals and other institutions. Of course a lot of the money was spent and the increase in retail sales caused the huge rise in GDP growth.

The fact that this retail sale growth caused only a modest up tick in core inflation, from 1.9% to a peak of 2.4% before falling back to 2.2%, proves that the 'new paradigm' held true.

The Fed is still furiously draining the liquidity from the banking system in order to correct their over-zealousness. This action has slowed growth to 5.4% in the first quarter and GDP growth will be even slower in the second quarter of this year. This should be good news for everyone.

However, the Federal Reserve members should stop peddling the 'old paradigm' nonsense as the reason for raising rates. Alan Greenspan's job is safe for another four years therefore he should only raise interest rates to resolve the problem that the Fed created, tell the truth, and stop insulting our intelligence.

Don't forget that President Clinton called a White House conference on April 5th with business leaders and economists. They discussed the policy questions growing out of the shift into a 'new paradigm'. It was about time that someone explained it all to the 'old paradigm' economists.

We continue to explain it like this:

- once upon a time, strong growth led to inflation.
- inflation is 'bad'.
- some people mistook this to mean that strong growth is 'bad'.
- the link between strong growth and inflation was eventually broken.
- now we can have strong growth without inflation.

The reason that the 'old paradigm' economists will not admit this is that they recognise that in the 'new paradigm' an economist is about as useful as a weatherman in the Sahara!

We should all remember that what makes America such a great country is that it was "*a new nation conceived in liberty and dedicated to the proposition that all men are created equal.*"

Any person entrusted with leading such a great country should bear in mind that they are tasked with ensuring that "*government of the people, by the people, for the people, shall not perish from this earth.*"

With this spirit in mind, Alan Greenspan was recently asked to explain in a letter to Congress, whether or not interest rate policy was being conducted to rein in the rise in equity prices.

He answered that it was not his role to target equity prices and that monetary policy was solely directed towards controlling inflation.

New Paradigm

Our analysis shows that the Fed did not need to raise interest rates between June 1999 and March 2000, and only did so to appease a bond market that had moved to expect at least a 0.25% rise on each occasion. The bond market was wrong in its view.

If the Fed had not moved, the bond market would have fallen, pushing long-term interest rates higher on the fear that the Fed was "*behind the curve.*"

Low unemployment, strong growth and strong retail sales do not automatically lead to higher inflation. As long as consumers continue to need lower prices to entice them into spending then the strong growth, low inflation environment will continue.

This constant need for lower prices stems from continued job insecurity. Despite strong growth and the low unemployment rate, a recent Federal Reserve-sponsored survey found a higher level of job insecurity than existed during the depths of the 1991 recession.

Paradoxically, this insecurity is a direct result of the record economic expansion.

The long economic expansion and the absence of the old 'boombust' roller coaster continues to encourage an increase in business start-ups. This leads to more companies competing for employees as well as competing for customers. The competing firms then bid up wages for employees. However, this will not lead to inflation because the same competition between firms is bringing down the prices of goods and services.

The squeeze caused by higher employment costs and a lack of pricing power means that firms must raise productivity in order to maintain profit growth. This increase in productivity increases the amount of goods and services on the market, which completes the virtuous circle causing this unprecedented period of strong growth and low inflation.

The evidence for this is there for all to see in the personal computer (PC) market. PC sales are up dramatically (an increase in consumer spending), but only because the unit prices are falling and in some cases PCs are being given away.

All this processing power is being used by businesses to increase productivity, and by consumers to search the Internet for the best prices for goods and services.

We therefore have increased productivity, leading to increased wages, leading to increased retail spending, leading to falling inflation.

What must be remembered is that Alan Greenspan is the *Chairman* of the Federal Reserve but he only has one vote. His public comments therefore *must* recognize the views of the other Federal Reserve Board members even if he does not agree with them.

However as Chairman, he does have significant influence and fortunately he is firmly in the camp of the believers in the 'new paradigm'.

  May the good times continue to rock and roll…!!

The first quarter of 2000 was an important time for the United States economy. The worst concerns about the impact of the Y2K bug had not come to fruition. The economy had grown by 4.3% in 1998 and by 4.2% in 1999 but the core rate of inflation still fluctuated around the 2.4% level. It is at this point that the 'goldilocks' scenario of strong growth and low inflation had been realized. The 'goldilocks' economic scenario describes an economy that is not too 'hot' to ignite inflation, nor too 'cold' to cause stagnation. The US economy had been expanding since 1992 and had been creating jobs at a record rate. The unemployment rate had fallen to below 4.0% and everything in the wider economy seemed to be functioning perfectly. This economic performance was the verification of 'rock and roll economics.' The American people had organized themselves to their own advantage without the help of the Federal government and were doing just fine thank you very much. Unfortunately whilst the wider economy was functioning well, over on Wall Street it was a completely different picture. The economists in the Wall Street investment banks and in certain government agencies were beginning to worry. These economists never believed in the 'goldilocks' economy and they had taken great pains to say so. In fact, it may not be unfair to say that some people had staked their careers on the fact that 'goldilocks' did not exist, could not exist, and that anyone who claimed otherwise was dismissed as a new age crank.

However, there was a problem in the wider economy that had not been resolved completely. The matter of the Y2K bug was having an unfortunate hangover effect. The Y2K bug was the computer system problem related to the change in date from 1999 to 2000. Many computer systems had been designed only to accept a year entry in the format of 'yy'. This meant that dates such as 1996 would be abbreviated to 96. Normally this would not have been a problem but the advent of the new millennium meant that the year 2000 would be abbreviated to 00.

Again initially, there is not really a problem. However the problem arises when the date is used in a calculation. For example, a credit card issued in 1996 to expire in four years time would have an expiry date of 00. Unfortunately the abbreviation would assume that the 00 date was in fact 1900 and the computer system would think that the card had in fact expired some ninety-six years previously. The potential impact of this problem, especially in the financial sector, was huge. The banks feared a drain on liquidity in the event that worried customers withdrew funds just in case the banking system was out of action.

To avert this potential liquidity crisis the Federal Reserve pumped liquidity into the banking system so that the banks would have funds to draw against if necessary. Unfortunately, it appeared that the banks, upon realizing that customers were not withdrawing funds, merely drew down on the Fed liquidity in any case. This liquidity found its way to other institutions and individuals by way of short-term borrowing. For instance, the amount of trading taking place on the Nasdaq stock exchange using margin accounts ballooned. It appeared that the stockbrokers were encouraging their clients to speculate with borrowed money. This kind of manic action is usually seen at market peaks such as 1929 and 1987. This margin trading only served to stir up an already over-heated Nasdaq market and of course the Nasdaq crashed when the margin loans were called in. The Nasdaq stock market peaked at 5050 on March 10 2000 and at the time of writing it is around 1550, some 70% lower than the peak.[10] The United States economy that had been 'rocking' to the envy of the rest of the world had now peaked and had begun to start 'rolling'. The policy mistakes had, for the most part, already been made and the damage had been done. Now the US economy would start to unravel in Hollywood style slow motion.

---

10. The time of writing is May 2003.

Commentary—September 2000

Well, well, well. What a year! As of July, SIC Global was up 10.4% against 4.3% for the Nasdaq, 2.8% for the S&P500, and a miserly -5.9% for the Dow Jones Index.

In a six-month period that has seen some of the best investors in the world fall by the wayside, SIC has gone from strength to strength. Julian Robertson, George Soros, and Warren Buffett have all thrown in the towel on an endeavour that continues to tax the best and brightest minds in the world.

That's too bad! Now there's a new king in town and Wall Street is sitting up and taking notice.

What makes the stock market so difficult at this time is that there are still many stocks traded on the Nasdaq that are not even real businesses. To say that these stocks are *"overvalued"* is to imply that they even deserve to have a price. Some of these stocks should be trading at zero…and you know which ones we mean.

During the 1998–2000 period the Nasdaq market experienced a level of fraud that is unprecedented in American financial history.

Venture capitalists, company executives, brokers, fund managers, and journalists have all conspired to collectively defraud the American investor out of trillions of dollars. Those individuals and institutions that still hold these stocks should dump them now, before they go to zero, and call their lawyers.

So you think that fraud is too strong a word for it. We don't. Fraud is defined as *"obtaining money by deception"*.[11] The brokerage firms involved in the IPOs that brought these stocks to the public markets failed in their duty to ensure that they were viable businesses.

---

11.   This is a standard dictionary definition. The Oxford Dictionary of Law
      expands on the definition by stating that is a *"false misrepresentation by means of
      a statement or conduct made knowingly or recklessly in order to gain material
      advantage"*

They might claim that the investors should have done their own "*due diligence*" but as the big-tobacco cases are proving, a warning on the packet (read prospectus) is not sufficient indemnity when the product (read business) is not viable.

The US economy is a runaway train right now…and runaway trains don't just slow down by themselves…they crash. They crash killing everyone on board!

The SIC 'new paradigm' theory leads to faster and faster growth with lower and lower inflation. The inflation that is evident now is only a result of rising oil prices. If the rising oil price is reversed then the inflation disappears. However, if the rising oil price is not reversed then the Fed must raise interest rates further to slow the economy.

The strong growth, low inflation 'miracle' is blinding investors and economists to the fact that there are no brakes in this 'new paradigm'. It cannot be controlled. Some might say that it is post-modernism, but we say that it's just they way life is. If you don't like it there's always an easy way out.

"My my, hey hey…rock and roll is here to stay…"

'Rock and roll economics' accepts that boom will always lead to bust; therefore it is better for the authorities to intervene *before* the boom gets out of control. It shows a lack of understanding of the human condition for the central banks to intervene after the event and to blame the economic participants for their folly. The better action is to let the economic participants make their own decisions but to be on the look out for the actions of the 'rock and rollers' who will always seek to cause trouble. If these 'rock and rollers' are stopped early enough, before they can unleash too much of their brand of economic mayhem, then the boom/bust phenomenon can be stopped in its tracks.

If the central bankers had understood the concept of 'rock and roll economics' they would have spotted the deliberate attempt by OPEC to scupper the US economy by raising oil prices in the early 2000s as it did in the mid-1970s. It was cold, calculated, and clear for everyone to see. The Arab 'rock and rollers' were back and this time they would not be content with merely causing a world recession.

The following is an extract from www.solomon-investments.com written in February 2001.

Oil Prices—February 2001

Oil has more than tripled in price since December 1998 and is continuing on its seemingly relentless rise. A quadrupling of the oil price in 1973–4 caused a huge recession with a resultant bear market that took stocks down 40% at their lows. Last year the Nasdaq Composite fell almost 50% from its highs, and a 40% fall from its highs would leave the S&P 500 slumped at 900!!

Are you prepared? We are. Invest with solomon-investments.com and you will profit in all market conditions, even 40% bear markets!!

It is not necessarily our view that it *will* happen, but it is our job to know that it *could* happen. Is it happening now, right in front of your very eyes? Read on and decide for yourself...

In an apparent attempt to prevent the above situation, OPEC decided in March, June, and September of 2000 to increase oil production in order to offset the supply-demand imbalance. This was supposedly intended to push oil prices back into the $22–28 per barrel target range.

However, after brief falls in April and July, prices rebounded and moved higher. This shows that the oil market is proving resistant to all attempts to stop the upward trend in oil prices.

We wonder what the new Energy Secretary Spencer Abraham will do now that OPEC are pumping all the oil that they can drill but prices continue to rise. Former Energy Secretary Bill Richardson's answer was to plunder the US strategic oil reserves but that only provided a fleeting respite.

OPEC has since admitted that the present situation of 'full capacity' with ever rising prices is a dream come true for them. At the same time it has turned into a nightmare for the rest of the world. Even after the fuel protests in Europe, and the energy crisis in California, it is clear that the nightmare is not yet over.

After the recent decision to reduce production, and the prospect of more production cuts, it is increasingly apparent that OPEC is waging a *jihad* against the United States. We should all bear in mind that most Arab nations find the American economic and political system totally reprehensible, and that their protestations regarding the need for *"stable oil prices"* is merely empty rhetoric that may indeed mask a much more sinister motive.

In the early 2000s, just as it was in the 1970s, only a few groups were causing trouble. Unfortunately they were causing a lot of trouble. When the 'rocking and rolling' started to affect the wider economy, the Federal Reserve members had many choices. They chose *not* to intervene and left the stock market regulation to the Securities and Exchange Commission (SEC). They chose *not* to raise margin requirements to tackle the source of the problem directly. They chose instead to jawbone incomprehensively about *"irrational exuberance."* This highlighted the ineffectiveness of standard economic models against a concerted attempt by a few 'rock and rollers' to derail an entire economy for the sole purpose of lining their own pockets. In 'rock and roll economics' this kind of action is expected and anticipated once the economy has been growing for a few years. It is expected that the SEC will be ineffective against the abuses because the regulatory bodies would by definition be part of the problem. Whether by incompetence or by bribery, it should be expected that the 'rock and rollers' will be able to steer themselves around whatever regulatory regime is in place. This is in a similar way that a gang of burglars must by definition find a way around the security system in order to accomplish their goal. 'Rock and roll economics' is the insurance that allows the economy to sleep at night; rest assured that no financial loss occurs from any breach of security.

Meanwhile, the stockbroker and fund management complex on Wall Street was desperately trying to keep the stock market rising. They were only concerned with capital appreciation, even at the expense of the integrity of the market itself. It was not always like this because once upon a time, the receipt of a dividend was the main purpose of stock investing and any capital gain was the icing on the cake. Over a period of time the push for growth took over and companies moved away from issuing dividends. The companies instead undertook policies designed for share price appreciation. The investment funds then stopped requesting dividends and the newer investors assumed that ever rising share prices was the norm. It is this thinking that led to the Nasdaq fraud of 1998–2000.

While this was happening, over in Washington Federal Reserve chairman Alan Greenspan was, and still is, putting the cart before the horse in a similar way to some of the dot-com entrepreneurs. He is attempting to manage the economy in the same way that companies like eBay sought to manage their share price. If a company is managed well, the share price should rise accordingly and conversely if it is managed badly. However, some dot-com entrepreneurs sought to implement management decisions designed to keep an over-inflated share price rising even higher. Alan Greenspan is trying to keep a long-expanding US economy growing long after dangerous signs of stress have occurred. His monetary easing in the face of the 1998 Asian crisis only helped to further inflate the over-valued stock market and lead directly to the bubble that was pricked so spectacularly in the crash of 2000. He is now pumping money furiously in order to prevent the recession that usually follows the pricking of such an excessive speculative bubble. The economy should be allowed to retrench somewhat in order to unwind the supply-side excesses. To inflate the economy now because inflation is historically low will cause inflation in the future that will require a huge recession to unwind it. This inflation is already rampant but it is not in goods, it is in assets such as land and houses. Unfortunately this inflation does not count as part of the official calculations but it is still inflation all the same.[12] Asset prices for one do not seem to count because the central banks still seem to be obsessed with a potential wage/price spiral.

Greenspan is obviously putting the management of his reputation before the management of the US economy. His success over his fifteen-year tenure has arguably gone to his head. This is unfortunate because he seems determined to secure his reputation as the greatest Federal Reserve chairman in United States history by leaving an even larger problem for his successor.

To summarize 'rock and roll economics' we must reiterate that standard economic theory assumes that people make rational economic choices—but this is patently false. Human beings, even the most high and mighty, make irrational decisions and mistakes of judgement. Even the economic decision makers in the central banks are not immune to the human condition. It was the struggle with the human condition that gave birth to rock and roll music, and it is the struggle with the human and economic condition that has given birth to 'rock and roll economics.' In the next chapter we will see how 'rock and roll economics' explains the current demise of the Anglo-American capitalist system.

---

12. Inflation is measured by using a basket of commonly purchased goods. Unfortunately there are many goods and services that are excluded from this basket. Therefore any inflation measure is by definition arbitrary.

5

Executive Compensation Syndrome

To really understand the technology stock boom and bust of the late 1990s one must look back in time to the stock market boom and bust a decade previously. At the time, the stock market crash of 1987 seemed catastrophic. However, by the mid-1990s it had been made to look like a small blip in an ever-upward rising stock market that promised to provide wealth and security for a new generation of investors and pensioners. These people saw their savings increase at a rate that far outstripped any other asset class.[1] This astronomical rise was fuelled to a large part by the ability of large corporations to obtain a far greater share of national output than they had enjoyed in the 1970s and the 1980s. From the perspective of the new millennium the outstanding question that needs to be answered is:

"Did the move towards stock option remuneration for top executives fuel the Nasdaq fraud?"

To answer this question one must get to the heart of what a stock option is and what it is not. A stock option grants the holder of the option the right to purchase stock in a company at a fixed price at some point in the future. The stock option will usually have an expiration

---

1.   From 1984–1998 the overall return from the Financial Times All-Share index, including dividends reinvested, was a remarkable 17.1% per year. By way of contrast the 100-year average return is 7% of which more than half was from dividends.

date before which the option must be exercised. To exercise an option, the option holder purchases the specified number of shares at the agreed price. The value of such an option depends upon three things. These three things are the strike price of the option, the market price of the underlying security, and the time left to expiry. Depending on the balance of these factors, the stock option itself is either an incentive to drive company performance, a worthless piece of paper, or a license to print money.

The appeal of stock options to executives is quite obvious, but before we can examine the appeal in detail one must examine the motivation of the recipients of the stock options. Despite the enormous salaries paid to top executives in recent years, and especially in the United States, one must remember that the executives belong to the middle-classes. It must be borne in mind that the middle-classes are essentially a lazy lot. Let us not mince words. They are, as a whole, bone-idle. If one were to ask a group of middle-class people to do something to earn a reward the silence would be deafening. Conversely if one were to offer them an opportunity to get something for nothing one would get trampled in the rush. It is this almost genetic desire to get something for nothing that truly defines the middle-class and sets them apart from the other classes in the Anglo-American class structure.

It is from amongst the top performers of this class that a corporation's top executives are drawn. The owners of the businesses that employ these executives assume some degree of uncertainty in the hope of achieving an above average return on their investment. However when it comes to motivating top executives, using such an approach would be doomed to failure. Quite frankly, if remuneration were based on quantified performance with the understanding that failure would be punished by financial loss, it would be impossible to find any takers for even the most prestigious of executive positions. It is because of this lack of motivation that the use of stock options as a performance incentive gained in popularity during the late 1980s. Unfortunately, the popularity of stock options encouraged a culture of over-extending companies in the hope of share price appreciation without any care for downside risk. Executives were being rewarded for good performance without being penalised for negative performance. Such a skewed remuneration system almost guarantees the development of a boom/ bust situation to the eventual detriment of the owners of the business. The risk is borne totally by the business owners because if the company suffers financial catastrophe the failing executives merely leave the mess for someone else to clear up.

The trend towards stock options and the urge to create shareholder wealth was driven by the twin concepts of 'Gordon Gekko' and the *"greed is good"* culture. 'Gordon Gekko' is the fictional character from the 1987 film Wall Street that was based on an amalgam of several real-life characters populating Wall Street at the time. The ruthless nature of his business dealings, his willingness to cut corners, and to break the law was intended to create a character that represented the worst of capitalism. 'Gekko' was a gloating, bloated, monster of a character that was the evil embodiment of rampant self-interest. Unfortunately what was supposed to be an anti-hero creation of the director Oliver Stone became instead a role model for business dealings both inside and out-side Wall Street. 'Gekkoism' has ruled the Anglo-American economies since the late 1980s. It has nothing to do with monetarism or any other of the well known economic dogma that has stifled intellectual debate and government policy over the last thirty years. It is based on greed—nothing more and nothing less than pure greed.

'Gordon Gekko' may well have been a creation of the 1980s but he never really went away. Unfortunately, it is not clear whether people revere him or revile him. 'Gekko' claimed that corporate executives were under-performing and that their job was to create wealth for the company's shareholders. In the late 1980s, corporate raiders used financial leverage to release the 'hidden value' in corporations. These corporate raiders were adept at finding companies where the whole was worth less than the sum of the parts. The aim was to buy the whole company with borrowed money in the form of 'junk' bonds, and sell off or 'un-bundle' selected parts of the corporation to repay the debt. This exercise would leave the corporate raider with a profit from the various sales, plus ownership of the profitable core business.[2]

The corporate executives of the late 1980s were frightened by 'Gordon Gekko' and became focused less on running their businesses and more focused on the perceived value of the business as measured by the share price. This fear-induced focus was deliberate and was intended to ensure that the executive delivered value to the shareholders rather than waste the company's money on empire building and executive perks. Unfortunately the method of achieving this focus, namely executive stock options, became the ultimate company perk. As time went on it became increasingly difficult to grow businesses so that by the late 1990s a new breed of executives resorted to fiddling the accounts to keep the share prices rising. Running a business in a modern supply-side economy is very difficult because profit must come at the expense of another company. It follows that all companies cannot win. Once companies ceased to be undervalued in relation to their assets, it became harder to grow companies organically. Generating profit by selling assets is easy. Generating profit by acquisition is also easy. However growing the business by producing and selling better products and services is much more difficult.

It is in the combination of huge risk-free rewards for presiding over share price appreciation allied with an extremely competitive business environment that the seeds of the late 1990s Nasdaq fraud were sown. The goal of stock option remuneration was to give executives an incentive to negotiate the stormy waters of international business. It was meant to encourage executives to *"think the unthinkable"* in the search for corporate value. Instead, the middle-class executives in charge of

2.   *"Takeover"*

corporate America reverted entirely to class stereotype and merely sought ingenious ways of gaining the value of generous stock options without actually managing the corporations in order to generate the economic value that would justify such remuneration packages.

'Gordon Gekko' had arrived, and the wheels had been set in motion for 'Gekkoism' to supplant all previous established economic and business logic. To fully understand 'Gekkoism' fully one must take selected 'Gekko' quotes from the film "*Wall Street*" and analyze them critically.

"The illusion has become real, and the more real it becomes, the more desperate they want it."

Paul Krugman claimed in his book "*Peddling Prosperity*" that the economic boom of the late 1980s was all a mirage.[3] He argued that politicians and economists created economic growth that was nothing but an illusion. However the illusion began to be realized in the late 1990s. The strong growth and low inflation environment that had been hitherto unattainable had in fact been achieved from 1996 onwards. Unfortunately the Federal Reserve 'misjudged' monetary policy in the summer of 2000 and triggered the Nasdaq crash before the overheating stock market had a chance to correct itself. It can be argued that the path of economic growth would have continued if the Federal Reserve had not intervened with interest rate rises in order to prick the technology stock bubble. By March 2000 the Nasdaq bubble had already begun to deflate by itself and the Federal Reserve induced interest rate raises only served to bring a halt to the economic expansion in the wider economy.

---

3.   "*Peddling Prosperity*"

"Money itself isn't made or lost, it's simply transferred, from one perception to another."

The most basic rule of financial markets is that for every buyer there must be a seller. In the ever-increasing complexity of modern international markets it is easy to forget this simple fact. Adam Smith states that the amount of money circulating in the economy cannot increase without an increase in productivity; however, most transactions in the financial markets merely involve moving money from one place to another.[4] It is only when a product is sold at a profit that money is actually made. This is not the case in the financial markets because no real products are actually being sold. In fact, the only products being created are ever more esoteric financial instruments that provide little or no value to the purchaser but whose only purpose is to profit the investment bank selling the instrument. Unfortunately the ingenuity of the inventors means that the destructive nature of these financial instruments is not immediately apparent. However the danger usually becomes clear after some headline grabbing financial disaster that reveals in hindsight the folly of corporate executives, investors, and even more so, the government regulators designed to protect the public.

"A fool and his money are lucky enough to get together in the first place."

Money is hard to make and even harder to keep. This is true today and has always been true because there are so many crooks, criminals, sharks, and charlatans whose sole purpose in life is to relieve the gullible public from their hard earned cash. Unfortunately white-collar theft still goes relatively unpunished. This is because white-collar crime is in effect middle-class crime, and it is the middle-class that operates

---

4. *"Wealth of Nations"*

the legal system. The middle-classes have used this class power to de-criminalize white-collar crime. White-collar crime is rampant in the banking system and still goes relatively unpunished. Once upon a time people placed their money with the banks in order to protect them from thieves. Then the thieves turned to blowing safes and robbing the banks. Now it seems that the bank robbers are actually working within the banking system itself and seek to steal the depositors' money by stealth.

"The public's out there throwing darts at a board. I don't...I bet on sure things."

The financial markets have a low barrier to entry for participants. On the other hand, the financial institutions themselves have a high barrier to entry for participants. The remuneration packages offered by the big banks attract bright graduates from the best universities in the world. This mismatch of expertise is designed to work to the advantage of the institutions controlling the financial markets. Bearing in mind the fact that the stock market is a zero-sum-game, the market returns gained by the institutions must come at the expense of the other players.[5] It follows that the institutions as a class earn their returns from the legions of individual investors. The individual investor is encouraged to buy and sell individual stocks that are tipped to rise in the near future for some reason or another. The individual is not encouraged to research in any great detail the stocks that they buy and sell. In fact they are positively discouraged from doing so. The idea is promoted that buying a stock for it to appreciate in price and then selling it for a profit is somehow not only easy but can be done successfully by anyone who can open a brokerage account and is willing to trade for between $5 and $25 per trade.

---

5.   *"Winning The Losers Game"*

On the other hand the institutional investor benefits from the knowledge gained by research analysts employed by the brokerage firms. These analysts do not however analyze the companies to which they are allocated. The analysts are appointed because of friendships with key executives at the relevant companies. The analysts use these friendships to gather inside knowledge of earnings expectations that are then passed on to the clients of the brokerage houses in exchange for commission on the trades. The analyst recommendations that are made public do not contain anything of value to the individual investor. The institutions know to ignore this so called research or merely to take it with a pinch of salt. It can therefore be argued that not only is the analyst recommendation a fraudulent deception but also that the excess commissions generated by the investment funds in exchange for the insider information is in fact a theft from the owner of the business. These business owners are the customers of the pension funds and insurance companies that hold the stock. One answer to this conflict of interest is for the investment funds to undertake independent research and allow the brokerage houses to focus on buying and selling the required stocks at the best possible price. Alternatively, and increasingly in this age of outsourcing, another answer is for the investment fund to buy in the services of a third-party research firm. The fact that the research firm or investment fund might employ similar tactics to those currently employed by the brokerage houses is neither here nor there. The services will be paid for directly; therefore there will be no conflict of interest between the brokerage houses and both the individual and institutional investors.

"I look at a hundred deals a day, I choose one."

Whether one believes in the Efficient Market Hypothesis (EMH)[6] or not, the fact is that the investment markets in the larger western economies provide few opportunities for profit on a balanced risk-reward basis. The fact that one must first outlay capital in the gamble, calculated or otherwise, of a profit over and above the initial outlay plus commission charges, means that the market participant must be quite sure that the investment will be fruitful. It is quite obvious that the most fruitful opportunities will be soon picked clean by the most nimble of participants if not already consumed by eager insiders. Therefore it must be quite clear that on any given day in a remotely efficient market, the opportunities for successful investments must be few and far between. Equally obviously, it does not benefit the brokerage houses to declare the fact that it would in all probability, be better not to bother. Stockbrokers therefore continue to tout the latest hot deal or mispriced security in the hope of gaining more commission. Unfortunately for the market participants they must continue to analyze these bogus profit opportunities in order to find the ones that are real. However the best profit opportunities must by definition be few and far between.

"Wonder why fund managers can't beat the S&P 500?...Because they're sheep, and sheep get slaughtered."

When sheep are on the move they tend to follow the leader. Experiments have shown that when a flock of sheep is presented with a hurdle, the leader will jump over the obstacle and the rest of the flock will follow accordingly. This all seems reasonable but it all becomes peculiar when the hurdle is removed. The sheep continue to jump at the spot where the hurdle was previously situated. The rest of the flock

---

6.   Efficient Market Hypothesis claims that market movements are random and cannot be predicted.

continue jumping, as the previous sheep did, even when there is no apparent need to do so. Although the financial markets have always been susceptible to herd-like activity, it is the peculiar habits of the sheep that can only describe the actions of the institutional investor. It has also been remarked that the goal of institutional investing is like that of the judge in a beauty contest whereby the purpose is not to pick the most attractive contestant but to pick the contestant whom one thinks the other judges will find attractive.[7] Therefore it does not behold a judge or investor to be too brave in making a selection for fear of being incorrect. The fact that the largest profit will accrue to the investor making the first move is countered by the fact that if the move is incorrect the net result will be much worse. This is because correcting the error will encounter capital loss and increased commission charges. The conservative approach is therefore to wait until one of three things happen:

- Enough insiders make their moves content in the knowledge that they know the result beforehand.

- Enough brave investors make their moves early so that it is clear that the voting so far is so compelling as to effect the end result no matter how foolish it may appear. This was the reaction of the institutional investors as the dot-com fever reached its peak. The Motley Fool-type individual investors had pushed prices so high, and were continuing to rack up huge paper gains, that the institutions were forced to pile in or risk having the money redeemed for underperformance.[8] The fate of the Phillips and Drew fund manager Tony Dye was a classic example of what can happen. His sacking compelled other fund managers to sim-

---

7. JK Galbraith and Benjamin Graham.
8. See www.fool.com for details of the way individuals were ironically led to behave in the late 1990s. It appeared to be working but was merely building a pyramid scheme that would eventually collapse.

ply follow the herd. It was more than their jobs were worth not to play along.

- If no one makes a move then the fund manager does not need to make a move. The company concerned may well be the best company in the world with fantastic growth opportunities but if one's peers are not investing, then the fund manager is not punished if he or she does not invest. It is an asymmetrical risk-reward proposition that often leads to worthy companies going without financing whilst companies with a good following have access to much more money than they need. This over-funding of selected companies has the tendency to lead to sub-standard financial performance due to the inability of the company concerned to find worthwhile investment opportunities for the excess capital.

The telecom crash that occurred soon after the dot-com crash in the summer of 2000 was a great example of too much money chasing too few potential customers. The mismatch of supply and demand almost guaranteed that the expected returns would never be realized, and this lead to huge amounts of money being wasted. Adam Smith highlighted the tendency for companies to compete themselves to ruin once their number increases beyond the ability of the market place to sustain them. However in the case of the telecom crash and dot com crashes, one must replace "*wasted*" with "*defrauded*" as it has become clear that many of the business opportunities being promoted were never viable businesses in the first place, but were merely vehicles for opportunists to take advantage of the naïve investors who had recently been enticed into the market.

The result of this sheep-like activity is to confine the majority of institutional fund managers to chronic underperformance. As the percentage of assets under the control of the institutions has increased over the years the institutions have come to dominate the stock market. They have, in essence, become the market. The problem with such dominance is that it is logically impossible to out-perform oneself and the institutions have found themselves in the position of charging fees for performance that can be easily exceeded by an index tracker at much less cost.

*"Most of these Harvard MBA types don't add up to dog-s**t."*

Warren Buffett the billionaire investor claims that what is taught in business schools is not worth knowing.[9] Mark McCormack, the founder of IMG the global sports management company also claimed that the essence of business is not complicated and is not taught in business schools.[10] McCormack made the point that there is a gap between a business school education and the 'street knowledge' that comes from the day-to-day experience of running a business. Business school students by definition can only learn what can be taught. Unfortunately many of the important aspects of business, and especially the key components for success, cannot be taught. Although an advanced education can help, it is no substitute for day-to-day experience, and at worst it can induce a sense of naïve arrogance. McCormack termed the missing ingredient 'street smarts' and the concept is very much applicable to the financial markets. For once upon a time, the stock market thrived as a sort of gentleman's club. However, it has developed over time to embrace new products traded by an altogether different breed of person.[11] In the 1980s even Goldman Sachs the venerable blue-blood investment bank had bought into the *"greed is good"* culture and by the 1990s was actively competing with its own clients in areas such as risk arbitrage.[12]

---

9. *"Buffet Speaks"*
10. *"What They Do Not Teach You At Harvard Business School"*
11. See *"Liars Poker"* on the type of staff who populated the Salomon bond desk in the 1980s. They were loud, brash, and definitely did not attend Harvard Business School.
12. *"When Genius Failed"*

The problem of the missing 'street smarts' is brought about by the fact that the elements of investing as defined by Benjamin Graham are seldom taught in business schools because they are not complex enough.[13] Business schools reward complex decision-making rather than simple decision-making, but simple decision-making is quite often more effective. However, business schools are very important because many employers use them as a filtering system in order to make the employment process less error-prone. Unfortunately the effect has been to produce a generation of managers known more for their meddling mediocrity than their money-making abilities.

"They're analysts, they don't know preferred stock from livestock."

Analysts were once the poor relations of Wall Street. They provided a useful, if not highly regarded function. They produced detailed company analysis that would highlight companies of interest for investors. As it has already been stated however, the realities of fund management dictate that detailed analysis of a company is near worthless unless other funds are buying the stock. It is because this is true that having detailed fundamental knowledge of the company is not advantageous because the fund manager can merely follow the herd. However, original fundamental analysis and the insight gained from it, is useful at turning points in a company's fortunes. Unfortunately it is a brave fund manager indeed who will stake his career on the work of an analyst at these times.

To this end the work of analysts had always been held in relatively low regard. However, in the late 1990s the rate of pay of an analyst grew astronomically. Their power increased because of the ability to garner inside knowledge from companies about the likelihood or not of meeting the analyst expectations. The 'beat the estimates' game became the

---

13. *"Intelligent Investor"*

only way to keep an over-valued stock rising ever higher. In this way the analysts became key to the fund manager being able to invest safely in overvalued stocks and especially the technology stocks that were booming at the time. Beating the analyst expectations ensured that the company's stock price would rise after the quarterly results. The fund manager could therefore invest heavily secure in the knowledge that if the estimates were to be missed, his analyst would be given warning well in advance so that the fund could divest itself of the stock. The sequence of events often went like this.

- Analyst asks company executive "*will you meet the numbers?*"

- Company executive says to analyst "*estimates too high*"

- Analyst says to best clients "*sell now, as we need to downgrade*"

- Best clients sell, or buy puts to hedge exposure

- Analyst announces an 'earnings downgrade'

- Stock falls accordingly, usually by between 4–9%

- Best clients buy back the stock or sell puts at a profit

- Analyst expectations are now in line with the company's expectations

- Best clients accumulate more stock secure in the knowledge that the earnings estimates will be beaten

- Company announces earnings that beat expectations by a small margin

- The stock rises as individual investors and 'b-list' clients buy into the continuing growth story

- Best clients reduce exposure and take profits before the cycle begins again

This cycle seems benign and is well known within Wall Street but it can only succeed by deceiving the individual investor and the 'b-list' clients who are not party to the inside information gained by the analyst. At the present time analysts have ceased to analyze companies but instead undertake several roles that combine to produce the following effects:

- The analyst becomes a mole for the stockbroker garnering inside information

- Company gives inside information in return for investor exposure

- Investor exposure guarantees rising share price

- Rising share price guarantees company executive his/her job with perks such as lucrative stock options

- Rising share price also guarantees fund managers their returns and fees based on assets under management

- Upgrades and downgrades encourage churning of portfolios to benefit stockbrokers

The dramatic change in the nature of the role of the analyst was driven by the high valuation of stocks during the late 1990s. This rendered most tried and trusted methods of stock-picking unreliable at best and downright foolish in the worst cases. One outrageous example of blatant stock cheerleading was the case of Ralph Acumpora, the well-known analyst at Prudential Securities in New York. In 1999 he predicted that the Dow Jones Index would reach 13,000 by the end of 1999. When the stock market rolled over and his target was not reached he merely changed his prediction to Dow 13,000 by the end of 2000. He finally discredited himself with his call in March 2000 that the Nasdaq was going to reach 6000 very shortly.[14] He is now disgraced but has not disappeared. Analysts do not get sacked on Wall Street for being incompetent promoters. The analyst is merely given a back-stage role until such time that the gullible public can trust them again. In fact the dubious nickname given to this particular analyst namely "Ralph Make-em-Poorer" seems in hindsight not to be merely a piece of gentle teasing, but rather a very accurate description of the affect of analysts' recommendations upon anyone who adheres to them.

"The key to the game is your capital reserves. If you don't have enough you can't p**s in the tall weeds with the big dogs."

It is often said that in order to be a successful investor one must aim to "*buy low and sell high.*" Obviously the aim is to profit from the rise in price of the asset in question. The potential profit makes the project worthwhile and the worthiness of any investment must stand comparison with alternative investments available to the investor at the time. For a single investor this is a straightforward goal and the success or otherwise of any investment is dependant only upon the investor's ability to spot good investment opportunities. However, in the fund management arena the competition between fund managers compounds the problems for the investor. The fund manager must seek not only to profit from the investments, and a greater profit than from comparable investments, but he must also seek to generate greater profit than his or her fund management peers. Therefore in a market where security prices are constantly moving on breaking news or whispers, the ability to "*buy low*" is the key to out-performance. Unfortunately in a well developed, reasonably efficient market, any opportunity to purchase a security at a price that provides a good opportunity for potential profit will be seized upon very quickly. Therefore if a fund manager is to take advantage of these opportunities as they arise, the manager must have a ready supply of available cash. The manager of a hedge fund that has

---

14. The Nasdaq stock market is the US stock market favoured by high technology companies as it has less onerous reporting requirements than the New York Stock Exchange (NYSE).

the ability to borrow funds needs only to have a readily available borrowing facility and can use this leverage to generate excess returns. In contrast, the manager of a retail fund that has no borrowing capacity will need to have a portion of the fund in cash in order benefit from any good opportunities.[15]

Unfortunately during the bull-market of the late 1990s fund managers found themselves in a bit of a quandary because the near-efficient market provided few mis-pricing opportunities. The active funds that held cash were under-performing the passive funds that merely tracked an index. Therefore even if a fund manager found enough investment opportunities and was able to take greater advantage of them than his or her peers, the manager could still well under-perform the tracker funds and would have failed to justify the fund's existence. This led over time to a decrease in the proportion of a fund that was kept in cash. This increased the fund manager's relative performance in the short term but subsequently reduced the ability to profit from mis-pricing opportunities. To make matters worse, by reducing their cash holdings and buying the high-rising stocks in the technology boom, they were in fact contributing to the mis-pricing of stocks on the way up. This effectively removed the opportunity to profit eventually from the low priced stocks of well-managed companies that would inevitably become casualties as boom led to bust.

Therefore when the Nasdaq-inspired stock market crash finally occurred, it was short-selling and long/short hedge funds that were able to profit most from the crash itself and many other hedge funds managed to remain essentially flat amid a sea of falling indices and truly horrendous negative returns. It is during this time that hedge funds became seen to be the 'big dogs' in the investment jungle and their appeal widened. Fund management groups were forced to make hedge funds available to retail investors for as little as $10,000 where once an

---

15. See LTCM's facility with several banks and one in particular with Chase.

individual needed to be a 'high net-worth individual' with a minimum of $1,000,000 in assets.[16]

"You win a few, you lose a few, but you keep on fighting."

Life is a long-term game and many of the better prizes in the game of life accrue to long-term players. Although it is possible to amass a fortune in a short period of time, or to become an overnight success in the field of entertainment or sports, achievements such as these are relatively few and far between.

The usual route to success in any venture is the one of persistence and patience allied with talent. Edward de Bono's 1985 study of success and the tactics of achieving it identified four traits of successful people.[17]

- Single-mindedness

- Persistence

- Energy

- Determination

  ### *Single-mindedness*

  Single-mindedness is the ability to select a field of activity and to make that area the primary focus of attention. It stands to reason that at the higher levels of any discipline the competition will be so intense that any loss of focus will provide an opportunity for a competitor to take advantage of the situation at the expense of the less focused individual.

  This logic led to the 'unbundling' of conglomerates in the late 1980s as investors sought to reclaim shareholder value from

---

16. One example was the Xavier fund launched by Deusche Bank.
17. *"Tactics"*

companies that had become unfocused due to involvement in too many disparate businesses. Although the businesses may well have been related, it was shown that a company that was only focused on one area of business would be able to provide a much better service than a company whose focus was spread over many businesses. In his book "*The Wealth of Nations*", Adam Smith also emphases the importance of focus when referring to the division of work.

Persistence

Persistence is the ability to keep going despite encountering setbacks. It stands to reason that it is too much to expect to be successful at the highest level of one's chosen field, with flawless performances, without ever experiencing a negative event. It is therefore persistence that really sets the top-performing individuals, teams, and companies apart from their peers.

Energy

The ability to persist and to overcome obstacles is not possible without the energy to keep going. Money management is an extremely stressful and taxing discipline and one that is better suited to younger people. However the knowledge that comes with experience gathered over many years is extremely valuable. It therefore follows that those fund managers who have the most energy will be able to stay in the job for far longer than their less energetic peers. The experience gained in these later years will give the older fund managers an edge over their more energetic but less experienced counterparts. For example, the experience of negotiating bear markets is extremely valuable when a previous bull market turns negative. Likewise, when a previous bear market turns bullish. At these times the extra knowledge will enable the more experienced but still energetic fund managers to outperform their peers, and the less experienced and youthfully reckless managers will usually fall by the wayside.[18]

Determination

The determination to make an activity a success is the key attribute necessary to becoming a success. Determination provides the drive that lays the foundation for success that the attributes of single-mindedness, persistence, and energy is built upon.

To summarize de Bono, there are certain personality traits that help to achieve success. To obtain long lasting success one must identify a field of activity, and single-mindedly persist and drive the project from start to finish overcoming all obstacles. This study, and the conclusions drawn from it apply very well to the highly competitive world of business and investment.

"It's not always the most popular guy who gets the job done."

In many walks of life, there are difficult decisions to be made. However in business, the number of decisions and the impact of those decisions are much greater. The ability to make tough decisions when necessary will enable individuals possessing this trait to become more successful than their peers. For instance, the ability to *"buy low and sell high"* involves making unpopular decisions, the success of which will only become apparent over time.

---

18. *"Confessions of a Street Addict"*

"In my book, you either do it right or you get eliminated."

The 1980s saw the rise to prominence of the Darwinism ethos, that of *"the survival of the fittest."* The theory of natural selection is seductive for those seeking to promote a hands-off or laissez-faire attitude to government and economic policy. Darwin tried to show how nature evolved the diversity of species from common ancestry by way of selecting the species that best fit the environment in which it lived.[19] The species that did not fit the environment would not reproduce. However the species that was best adapted to the conditions would thrive and multiply. This survival of the species that best fit the environment was re-interpreted to mean that in a world of 'dog-eat-dog' it was the fittest dog that will win. In the 'rat race', the biggest rat will take the top prize. This is at best a misunderstanding of Darwin and at worst a deliberate misrepresentation of biological theory.

"Greed, in all its forms...cuts through and captures the essence of the evolutionary spirit."

Greed drives the need for more. This desire of humans to acquire and consume in turn drives the innovation of technology that increases economic productivity. This increase in productivity in turn creates an increasingly diverse range of consumer products. Each product cycle acts like a Darwinian environmental change that weeds out the weaker products and enables the consumer to gain greater customer satisfaction. This is all well and good but surely there is more to life than that.

---

19. *"The Origin of Species"*

"You're not naive enough to think that we're living in a democracy?..."

The following is an extract from the 'politics' page of www.solomon-investments.com first published in March 2001 and updated after the UK election in May 2001.

Does "Tony Blair PM" equal "I'm Tory Plan B"?

"You choose your leaders and place your trust,
as their lies wash you down and their promises rust..."
—"Going Underground", *The Jam*, 1980

Well it's the morning after the night when the pantomime circus known as the General Election came to town. Unfortunately the cracks in the facade were there for all to see.

How can we claim to live in a democracy when the turnout for the General Election was only 59%, and the Labour government won with only 43% of the vote? The political system means that the governing party has achieved its 'landslide' majority from only 25% of the voting population.

The Prime Minister is now free to use his majority in the House of Commons to implement any policy that he cares to put forward. The parliamentary system allows the government to totally disregard the 25% of the voters who voted for them, and the other 75% will have absolutely no say whatsoever.

This farce will be allowed to continue for up to five years before the whole circus starts over again. If this is democracy, you can keep it. It sounds like a tyrannical dictatorship to me.

"You'll see kidney machines replaced by rockets and guns,
and the public wants what the public gets..."
—"Going Underground", *The Jam*, 1980

To understand and to sum up 'Gekkoism' one must understand how one stakeholder group, namely the shareholders, sought to dominate the other stakeholders in corporate America and ultimately the wider economy. It stands to reason that a company's shareholders are an important stakeholder group and that they must have their objectives met. However it can be argued that 'Gekkoism' and the "*greed is good*" culture gave a justification for shareholders to override the needs of the other stakeholders and that this all-consuming greed has sown the seeds of the demise of Anglo-American capitalism as we know it. In the next chapter we will examine another important stakeholder in the fortune of a corporation. Bank financing is equally as important as equity financing and we can again use 'rock and roll economics' to examine the role of the lending banks.

6

The Genesis of Boom and Bust

The boom-bust cycle exists; this is a fact of life. It has been a feature of economics for as long as records exist. It is commonly supposed that booms and busts are caused by irrational activity on behalf of the participants in the economy. However, there is a case to answer that the institutions that are supposed to regulate the participants, in fact *cause* the boom and bust phenomenon.

We live in a capitalist society and the large banks control the banking system. It can be argued that the boom/bust cycle exists *because* of the banks. However before we can examine our modern capitalist economies we must remind ourselves what capitalism is and what it is not. The Oxford Dictionary of Sociology defines capitalism as:

> *"A system of wage labour and commodity production for sale, exchange, and profit, rather than for the immediate need of the producers."*

Now that we have cleared that up we can look at the banking system. The banking system, like the legal system, is populated by the middle-classes. As stated previously the primary goal of the middle-class is to get something for nothing. This attitude also permeates the banking system because banking is one of the primary middle-class professions. Basically the banks want to make money without taking any risks. The word 'risk' in this context is the economic definition of risk. In economics, 'risk' is defined as *"uncertainty of outcome."* It is a common misconception that the element of uncertainty is directly correlated with the potential for disaster. This is not necessarily true, as uncertainty does not always mean that a loss may occur. For example, a distribution of profits over five years of £100m, £150m, £250m, £160m, £120m shows a great deal of uncertainty but no loss has occurred.

This distinction is important to the understanding of how the modern economy works. These days many financial institutions are attempting to reduce or remove risk from their investment portfolios. Many new financial instruments such as interest-rate swaps, derivatives and mortgage-backed securities have been created by the large investment banks in recent years to enable their clients to better manage their risk profile. Unfortunately risk cannot be removed from the financial system as a whole. It is merely passed from institution to institution. One way of understanding this inability to eliminate risk is by referring to Newton's Third Law of Motion. Newton states that *"for every action there is an equal and opposite reaction."* When this law is applied to finance one can see that for every party there is a counter party. It therefore follows that the risk that one party is attempting to offset is merely absorbed by the counter party. As this counter party is by definition a part of the financial system, it follows that as a whole, economic risk cannot be eliminated from the financial system.

This inability of the financial system to eliminate risk causes tensions in the wider economy. The problem with the relationship between the banks and the wider economy is that economic theory states that an investor will demand a higher return for taking on greater risk. Therefore all things being fair and equal, the investors or businesspeople taking on the higher uncertainty over the business cycle should reap greater rewards. This is especially true since the risk involved also encompasses the risk of material loss. It must be accepted that risk is inherent is all aspects of life, and it is not possible to build and grow an economy without takings risks. This is the assumption that entrepreneurs recognize and act upon. They take risks in order to provide the goods and services that people want, at a price that they are willing to pay. They do this in the hope of profit. However they are willing to take a loss if the project fails. In this scenario, everyone in society gains. The consumers get the goods and services that they want at a price they are willing to pay. Investors get a reasonable rate of return on their investment. Employees get paid employment and financial security. Finally the entrepreneur gets ownership and control of the enterprise itself. It is only the lending banks that have a problem with this arrangement. The banks by definition have narrow profit margins and this is especially true when the banks lend to the most credit-worthy customers. The banks make their money by playing the 'yield curve'.[1] They borrow money for short-term repayment at the prevailing central bank base rate. They then aim to lend this money in the form of long-term loans at higher interest rates. Obviously this strategy assumes that the banks can find suitable customers willing to borrow this money with a reasonable chance that the money will be repaid. Unfortunately for the customers of the banks, the old adage that "*banks only lend you money if you can prove that you don't need it*" continues to hold true. When the economy grows for a long period of time, usually five years or more, the banks find that they make very good money. Unfortunately they do not make as much money as their risk-taking, product-producing customers. Banks as businesses in their own right do not like this. When the customers make good money and repay their loans, the customers find themselves not needing the banks. The customers do not need to borrow money and the banks find themselves needing to lend to less credit-worthy customers or face a reduction in profits. They are therefore forced to lend more and more money to increasingly less credit-worthy customers. This is in part because the most credit-worthy customers have already borrowed what they need to borrow at reasonable interest rates. Furthermore, the natural prudence of these good credit risks means that they are not inclined to borrow more

---

1.   The 'yield curve' is the curve on a graph that is shown when the differing bond yields are plotted against the different maturity dates.

than they can comfortably afford to repay. Therefore the banks extend their net to a wider customer base. This continues until everyone is drowning in debt, but it is acceptable because everyone is sure that the good times will continue. Furthermore, no one can see a reason why the good times should not continue. Unfortunately the good times will *not* continue, because the same lending banks subsequently urge the central bank to increase interest rates in order to slow down the economy.[2] These calls appear to be well meaning, but they are nothing short of profiteering in so far as it is the excessive lending that causes the boom to develop in the first instance. What the banks really mean is "*increase the profits on our existing loans, and transfer the wealth back from the economy.*" What happens in effect is that the banks' customers are borrowing against future earnings and these earnings are transformed into present earnings for the banks. When the banks stop lending to customers in order to finance current lifestyles from future earnings, the customers must retrench and reduce spending until the debt is cleared. At this stage the economy goes from boom to bust in one cynical instant.

Surely it is not outside the capabilities of modern central banks to find an answer to the perennial problem of the boom/bust cycle. Instead of increasing interest rates to slow the economy, it should be possible to increase the banks' capital ratios. The capital ratio of a bank is the ratio of assets to liabilities. Money that the banks lend goes on to the balance sheet as an asset. The money borrowed from the BoE to facilitate the banks' loans is accounted for as a liability. Therefore by raising the capital ratio and restricting the amount of money flowing into the money supply, the BoE can better contain over-lending by the banks. It is this

---

2. The UK Council of Mortgage Lending did this in June 2002 when the wider economy and the stock market turmoil pointed to the need for stable if not lower rates. Inflation was at 1.8% at the time and fell to 1.5% the following month. If inflation had fallen any lower the Bank of England Governor would have needed to write to the Chancellor to explain the divergence from the 2.5% target.

over-lending that is the root cause of recessions. If the banks want to make more money they should be encouraged to become more entrepreneurial. 'Rock and roll economics' accepts that people will always be inclined to over-borrow and to over-spend, and that the banks will always be inclined to under-invest and to over-lend. The central banks need to restrain the lending banks and allow the economies to grow in order to benefit all members of society. Of course, this all assumes that the central banks are in fact being run for the betterment of society as a whole and are not merely a tool of the ruling elite.

The envy that the lending banks' executives experienced during the late 1980s also infected the UK politicians in the 1990s and early 2000s. Career politicians who had embarked upon a life of pampered luxury at the expense of the taxpayer, a life thinly disguised as 'public service', suddenly found themselves financially worse off than their university peers who had sought careers in business and finance. They turned green with envy and collectively attempted to get a piece of the action. This rejection of principle in preference for profit was the spore that developed into the disease of sleaze that overran the Tory party in the mid-1990s. Lord Archer, Neil Hamilton and Jonathan Aitkin were all jailed for improprieties ranging from perjury, accepting cash for House of Commons questions, and not declaring corporate hospitality. These politicians broke well-established rules in a desire to enjoy the same trappings of success as enjoyed by their friends and university colleagues in business and finance. Unfortunately the Labour party, dubbed 'New Labour,' was even worse when it came to falling victim to temptation and bribery. Soon after coming to power in 1997, Peter Mandleson, Geoffrey Robinson, Keith Vaz, and even the Lord Chancellor Lord Irvine were guilty of *"mistakes of judgement"* that were as embarrassing to the public as they were to the government itself. Unfortunately, getting caught was the only *"mistake of judgement"* that occurred. As an old school master once said, *"do whatever you want but don't get caught."* However it seems that these days it is not even a crime to get caught.

The concept of 'rock and roll economics' is the antithesis to boom and bust. Policy-makers have tried over the decades to smooth out economic cycles in order to alleviate the distress caused by economic slumps. However, as the United States experience in the late 1990s showed, such attempts are doomed to failure. These vain attempts stem from the arrogance of policy-makers. This arrogance rivals that of King Canute who thought that he was the master of all that he surveyed and that he could command the waves. He stood on the shore and demanded that the waves retreat. They did not and he was swept away and drowned. History has demonstrated than whenever mankind tries to tame the forces of nature, mankind can achieve only a fleeting victory. The forces of nature are vast and extremely powerful. Nature, and especially human nature, will always win. The concept of 'rock and roll economics' is born of this fact.

To really demonstrate the culpability of the banks we will now look at the Russian financial disaster of 1998 and the role of Long Term Capital Management and the Wall Street investment banks that financed it. The Russian crisis almost brought down the entire United States banking system, and if it were not for the steep interest rate cuts by the Federal Reserve, the ramifications would have been truly devastating.

The Boom and Bust of Long Term Capital Management

An analysis of Long Term Capital Management (LTCM) shows how excessive bank lending has effectively destroyed the capitalist system, as we know it. Roger Lowenstein details the rise and fall of LTCM and shows how one small bank created a trillion-dollar hole in the US economic system.[3]

LTCM was a hedge fund in so far as it was an unregulated pool of money run on behalf of its partners. These partners were wealthy indi-

---

3.   *"When Genius Failed"*

viduals who, according to Securities Exchange Commission (SEC) rules regarding hedge funds, did not need the protection of regulators. LTCM did not engage in daring macro style bets in the way that George Soros did with his Quantum fund. The strategy employed by LTCM was in the old style of a hedge fund whereby LTCM sought to limit risk and volatility by hedging one security against another. LTCM would buy one security and sell a related security thereby profiting from the spread between the two. This form of trade is called arbitrage and it leads to steady if not spectacular profits. Successful arbitrage by financial participants has lead to the near-efficient nature of modern financial markets because professionals who do nothing else but keep prices of related securities in synchronization quickly seize upon mis-pricing episodes.

LTCM's specialization was in bond arbitrage. The aim was essentially to bet on the spread between pairs of bonds. As the bond prices move independently, the spread either widens or contracts. By betting on the spread itself rather than the movement of the individual bonds, LTCM's aim was to generate low risk profits. The fatal flaw in this strategy was that the LTCM models were based on an acceptance of the Efficient Market Hypothesis (EMH). This hypothesis states that markets are efficient in that the price of a security reflects all the available knowledge and therefore the security is correctly priced. If this were true there would be no profit to be gained by taking advantage of mis-priced securities. The fact that LTCM intended to trade away the discrepancies meant that any profit would be miniscule as a percentage of funds employed. This relatively low return on investment for a low-risk strategy is in keeping with efficient markets. The fact that LTCM boasted an ability to make *outsized* returns from a low-risk strategy meant that LTCM's claim could *never* have been true and the strategy, if executed as advertised, would have failed. It was only by leveraging the portfolio with the aid of bank borrowing that the outsized returns gained in the early years were generated. This borrowing meant that instead of LTCM being a low-risk hedge fund, it was in fact a very high-risk hedge fund that was deceiving its investors from day one. Looking even deeper, it may be asked why the partners in LTCM were eager to raise so much money at the outset. The $2.5bn that was raised was much more than any previous hedge fund launch when at the time a typical launch was one percent of that total. It may not be disingenuous to say that the sole purpose of the fund was to bamboozle investors with mathematics, thereby raising billions of dollars that the partners would take a share of by way of fees and employee expenses.

Furthermore it must be borne in mind that the primary motive behind the creation of LTCM was personal. The principal behind the fund was a former Salomon Brothers employee by the name of John Meriwether. His previous incarnation was as the idiosyncratic head trader of Salomon's Arbitrage Group (SAG). SAG was the blueprint for LTCM and had completed the cycle from initial success, to intoxicating outperformance, to gravity-reaffirming collapse, to dollar-cushioned disgrace. In addition to Merton and Scholes, the option-pricing professors, LTCM also recruited David W. Mullins, vice chairman of the US Federal Reserve and second in the Fed's hierarchy to the Fed chairman Alan Greenspan. LTCM was in effect a dream-team of 'rock and rollers.' The hedge fund was a 'rock and roll band' that would eventually shake the capitalist world to its very foundations.

The Wall Street bankers were bamboozled by the array of academic talent that LTCM had gathered together. It may be unfair to say that this was a deliberate attempt to swindle the banks, but it must be said that the organization of LTCM was unique in the history of Wall Street. The simple world of stock-broking had been transformed in recent years from a gentleman's club into a vicious contest of all-consuming ferocity in which money was the sole object and any tool that provided an edge was handsomely rewarded. In this environment the derivative products that were promoted by the investment banks were heavily sought after along with any individual clever enough to actually understand them without having the integrity to realize that they were useless instruments and extremely dangerous to the clients. In fact, putting derivatives in the wrong hands is like giving a chainsaw to a child.

It can be argued that David Mullins was acting out of self-interest and not in the interests of the United States economy when he urged Alan Greenspan to tighten interest rates in February 1994. When the Federal Reserve suddenly raised short-term interest rates it shocked the financial markets and caused credit spreads to widen. This widening of spreads worked to the advantage of LTCM. By May of that year the 30-year Treasury bond, the benchmark of government securities, had fallen by 16% taking the yield from 6.2% to 7.6%. The funds controlled by LTCM increased by 7% beginning a run of spectacular profits. The timing could not have been better and in hindsight what seemed like a verification of the partners' genius looks like either fortunate timing or insider trading at the highest level. This almost perfect start for the fund increased the level of the partner's confidence engendering a false sense of security that was ultimately to prove catastrophic.

The perfect start continued throughout 1994 as the turmoil in the bond markets that started in February created easy pickings for the LTCM strategy. It is in the nature of financial markets that large mispricing episodes take a long time to unwind. The traders who hold losing positions inevitably hope to break even and tend to hold on to losing positions for far longer than they should. Due to the volatile nature of markets there is a tendency in normal times for prices to fluctuate around certain price points. This usually provides traders with several opportunities to break even on a losing trade if they are able to hold on long enough. However during market meltdowns or market booms, it is possible for the markets to run away from traders who are holding on to losing positions. It is at these times that the big money is made. The losing traders who are desperately holding on for one more opportunity to break even are eventually frustrated, and are forced to capitulate at a far greater loss than the potential loss at which the inevitability of the loss became apparent. Once all the losing traders have closed out their losing trades, the profits to be derived from the prevailing trend start to diminish and the market will quickly return to a frustrating form of volatility that will try the patience of even the most skilled traders.

The widening of credit spreads after the tightening by the Federal Reserve meant that LTCM was able to profit from the reversal of the trend caused by the distress selling of competing funds. However LTCM was only able to capitalize on this discrepancy by borrowing huge amounts from the banks on Wall Street. In one of LTCM's earliest transactions it managed to execute a massive $2 billion dollar trade without using any of its own cash.[4] The fact that the Wall Street bankers were mesmerized by the array of talent and sophistication at LTCM meant that they failed to realize that LTCM needed the banks more than the banks needed LTCM. It was pure greed on behalf of the Wall Street executives that allowed LTCM to execute such highly leveraged trades. Worse still, these trades were hidden from the shareholders of the banks by being declared as off-balance sheet transactions. This meant that the profits from the Wall Street banks' dealings with LTCM were booked as income while the risk to the banks from which the profits were generated was hidden from the banks' shareholders. The upper echelons of Wall Street had always been an exclusive club but this club was now actively involved in taking massive gambles in the financial markets with shareholders money for the sole purpose of lining the pockets of executives via the one-way-bet that is executive share options. Furthermore, by not declaring the transactions on the balance sheet, it can be argued that the deliberate deception was yet another example of the executive fraud that was commonplace at the time.

---

4.   "*When Genius Failed*", p45

LTCM snared all of the major Wall Street banks in its web of leverage and secrecy. By not being dependant on any one bank, LTCM was able to play one bank off against another. The hedge fund took advantage of the hyper-competitive nature of Wall Street by forcing every bank to play along or risk missing out on the massive profit potential of the enterprise. This profit potential however could only be realized at the expense of competing arbitrage players. These other arbitrage players tended to be the proprietary trading desks of the Wall Street banks. Therefore it must have been obvious to the Wall Street executives that betting on LTCM was a de facto bet against their own banks.

LTCM never claimed to have any geopolitical experience that would give them a trading edge. The only advantage that LTCM ever claimed was the advantage of having superior knowledge of the mathematic models that were in vogue at the time.[5] LTCM's aim was to capitalize on market mis-pricing. Unfortunately this strategy assumes that the prevailing market price was *incorrect* and that LTCM was able to determine the *correct* price. This attitude smacks of extreme vanity. For a trader to claim that the market price is incorrect is tantamount to saying that the thousands of individuals who make up the market at any point in time have on aggregate made a mistake. That this happens from time to time is in the nature of markets. However for LTCM to base their trading methodology on the Efficient Market Hypothesis and then to claim that the market price is *incorrect* is an oxymoron. It must by definition be correct at the time if only to be proved incorrect in the future. It is unfortunately in the nature of financial markets to persist with seemingly irrational valuations for far longer than an individual trader can hold on to his or her trading position. This nature is due to the casino mentality of modern financial markets. As long as the players are using financial securities as gambling chips, the prices will be determined by the potential to profit from the actions of the other players. In this environment the price is irrelevant because it merely

---

5.   *"When Genius Failed"*, p55

acts as a point from which to measure profit or loss on any individual trade. This casino mentality is inevitable once investment has given way to speculation.

LTCM also used mathematics to predict the likely returns to investors. This seemingly sophisticated presentation merely amounted to guesswork. The calculations were based on historical bond prices. This method of calculating future prices is of course dependant on the assumption that the future will be the same as the past. Although this may seem a reasonable assumption, it is extremely hazardous in financial markets. The fact that so much computing power is dedicated to finding price patterns in historical data almost ensures that any such pattern will quickly become overused so that it ceases to work. The hedge fund also assumed that the volatility of the securities as calculated from historical data would remain constant.[6] This obviously cannot be the case. The fact that the prices of securities move on a daily basis as a result of news flow must surely have an impact on the volatility. Every time an event occurs that is outside of the historical range it would by definition expand the historical range in one direction or the other. Furthermore LTCM claimed that their trades were independent and that the chances of them all going sour simultaneously was next to zero. Unfortunately this again failed to take into account the nature of modern global financial markets. The participants in modern markets tend to play many financial markets simultaneously. They are looking for the best returns wherever they may be. Therefore if funds are withdrawn from one market it can quite safely be assumed that funds will be withdrawn from other markets. This global movement of funds means that markets that would historically have been uncorrelated are now very highly correlated. When one market crashes, they all crash.

LTCM showed absolute faith in their economic models. The partners had an almost messianic belief in their own abilities. Any dissenting

---

6. Volatility is the rate of change of the price of a security.

voices were quickly drowned out. This attitude shows all the hallmarks of 'groupthink'.[7]

In 1995 LTCM's bond arbitrage trades earned the hedge fund a 43% return after fees.[8] At the end of 1995, LTCM's equity capital had almost tripled to $3.6 billion with assets of $102 billion. However this capital base was not what it seemed. This was because the fund was leveraged twenty-eight to one. This meant that for every dollar of investors' money that the fund had under control it had borrowed another twenty-eight dollars from a variety of banks. When the 43% annual return is adjusted for the effects of leverage, the total return on assets was significantly less. If LTCM had not been able to borrow such large sums of money from other financial institutions the actual return to LTCM's investors would have been 2.45%. Furthermore, if all LTCM's derivatives trades were taken into account, its cash return was more likely less than 1.0%.[9] Not exactly a mark of financial genius. When leverage is used in this way it is an effective way of boosting returns, but it is very dangerous because leverage is a double-edged sword. Most successful traders and trading firms only use leverage sparingly and many traders do not use it at all. For most financial institutions excessive leverage is not worth the stress.

By the spring of 1996 LTCM had $140 billion in assets, a sum thirty times its underlying capital. It was at this time four times the size of the next largest hedge fund. In addition LTCM disclosed derivatives bets as at the end of 1995 on a total of $650 billion of securities. Banks were climbing over themselves to earn themselves miniscule margins

---

7. 'Groupthink' is the tendency for the various members of a group to try to achieve consensus. Where 'groupthink' is prevalent, the need for agreement takes priority over the motivation to try to obtain accurate knowledge to make appropriate decisions. This tendency has been suggested as being one of the prime reasons why politicians and business leaders operating in closed groups so often make disastrous decisions.
8. *"When Genius Failed"*, p77
9. *"When Genius Failed"*, p78

on their loans to LTCM. These loans were totally inappropriate given the implied risks and the potential return on investment. The bankers were lending recklessly and aggressively and as a result collectively creating a boom that would subsequently lead to bust.

By 1996, Merrill Lynch for example, was providing $6.5 billion of repo financing and proportionately more on the derivatives side. This total was roughly equal to Merrill's total equity. Merrill lent this money to LTCM in order to try to get to see LTCM's order flow. The ability to see LTCM's order flow would have been lucrative for Merrill Lynch because it would have opened the door to insider dealing and 'front running'. 'Front running' entails a stockbroker executing trades on its own account using the knowledge of the client trade that it has just acquired. When the client trade is executed the stockbroker quickly unwinds the position that it had taken on its own account and banks the profit. The customer loses out because the movement in the security price as a result of the stockbroker's trades in effect moves the price against the client. The fact that 'front running' is illegal is neither here nor there. It happens all the time and Merrill Lynch was hoping to be able to 'front run' LTCM's trades. LTCM was using the potential size of its business to negotiate preferential rates with the Wall Street banks but the banks seemed to overlook the fact that LTCM was only so powerful *because* the Wall Street banks were lending it so much money and doing business on such preferential rates.[10] It seems that the executives at the banks were also suffering from 'groupthink'.

By 1996 the partners' stake had grown to $1.4 billion. This was nine times the original $150 million investment. This spectacular return seemed to confirm the partners' genius but it was entirely due to the power of leverage. LTCM had massive borrowings. Its returns were entirely due to placing leveraged bets with other peoples' money. This is a further example of the kind of asymmetric risk-reward proposition

---

10. *"When Genius Failed"*, pp84–85

that the Wall Street executives and the middle-class partners at LTCM and were attracted to.

For LTCM's professors, Merton and Scholes, this financial success provided a scorecard that confirmed and validated their academic achievements. Unfortunately this was no more than intellectual vanity. The reality of the situation was that what Merton and Scholes knew was not worth knowing. It was only valuable because of the ability to convince others that the knowledge was valuable. Alchemists have always tried to turn lead into gold but modern day alchemists attempt to *persuade* you that lead *is* gold.

In 1996 LTCM's total profits were an amazing $2.1 billion. This total was more than many of the largest and most well known corporations in the United States. LTCM was still at this time, relatively unknown and highly secretive. This situation however could not continue. LTCM's $2.1 billion in profit was being transferred from other parts of the financial system and the wider economy. The institutions that were being drained of the $2.1 billion during 1996 were bound, at some point, to wake up and smell the coffee. It could *not* continue because LTCM produced no products and services from which consumers would benefit. Therefore once the losers on the other side of LTCM's trades realized what was happening, LTCM was bound to suffer a backlash. Competitors were setting up similar funds and forcing bond spreads higher. This influx of new money would benefit LTCM's trades in the short-term but in the longer-term it would remove the 'mis-pricing' that LTCM had exploited so successfully up to this point.

Newton 1 Black-Scholes 0

What goes up must come down, or so the saying goes. It is not always true of course but 'chaos theory' shows that simple systems do not necessarily contain simple dynamics. It was clear from the outset that the structure of LTCM contained contradictions that meant that the whole edifice was built on sand. The crux of the 'chaotic dynamic' inherent in LTCM's strategy was the claim that markets are *efficient* but LTCM was attempting to exploit the *inefficiencies*. Furthermore once these apparent efficiencies have been identified LTCM, by nature of the name if not anything else, expected to make long-term profits from the efficiencies. Modern markets are generally efficient precisely *because* it is notoriously difficult to generate long-term profits from market efficiencies. Once a technique or model is shown to generate excess returns it will quickly attract imitators. Whereas an industrial concern can obtain a copyright in order to protect innovation, financial trading techniques such as bond arbitrage cannot be copyrighted. Therefore it should have been expected that competitors would materialize if ever LTCM became hugely successful. The key word here is *if* because even the initial success was not guaranteed. It was only the fact that the Federal Reserve-induced market turn caused their competitors to lose money to the benefit of LTCM that made the performance of the hedge fund stand out from its peers. This initial success greatly aided by massive leverage made it seem to the outside bankers that the academic talent at LTCM was really onto something. Had the huge hedge fund not been clouded in intense secrecy, the real strategy of LTCM would have been obvious from the outset.

From a 'chaos' perspective we can see that LTCM contained from day one the same properties that would lead it to its enormous success and at the same time guarantee its eventual implosion. In the same way the early pioneers of 'chaos theory' were amazed at the way in which a plume of cigarette smoke rises upwards in an orderly manner before degenerating into total disorder.

It is the fact that the options professors overlooked the human factor that would trigger the decent into financial chaos. Once the markets that LTCM had successfully exploited were picked clean LTCM had to search for new markets and new opportunities to exploit. However, before we go further we can state quite clearly that LTCM did not *need* to pursue other opportunities. The partners at LTCM could have admitted quite easily that they had been luckier than they had originally anticipated and closed the fund when the profits in bond arbitrage became picked clean by the sheer number of new participants. The fact that LTCM needed enormous borrowings in order to produce any investor return worth speaking of should have been a red flag to a sane partner indicating that things were as good as they were ever going to get. The fact that there were no sane partners left at this point is again a result of the human condition that the options-pricing professors *ignored* on the way to the dramatic psuedo-scientific discovery on which they had built their academic careers.

Therefore when it all began to unravel it was most definitely 'chaotic.' However to be fair it must be said that the partners did indicate to investors that likelihood of investor returns continuing at the tremendous rate was slim and that the potential for material loss remained. Writing at the end of 1996 John Meriwether wrote:

> *"...the net return for 1997 is likely to be materially below the 1996 return...including the potential for loss."*

It can quite clearly be seen that the factors leading to the fall of LTCM were present within the factors leading to the success that preceded it. John Meriwether was correct in his prediction of potential disaster but he was one year early. LTCM would not blow up until 1998. However when it did the spectacle was well worth waiting for.

As stated previously the problems began when the run of outsized returns began to attract imitators. The Wall Street banks that had been lending enormous sums to LTCM were earning miniscule margins on their loans. When these banks started similar in-house operations along the lines of LTCM the good times were essentially over. What we must remember was that LTCM was only able to make their outsized returns *because* of the aggressive and reckless lending of the Wall Street banks. Of course the Wall Street banks wanted something for nothing and they were willing to lend large sums to LTCM because they believed the returns to be risk-free. It was therefore quite logical that these same banks would seek to emulate the success of LTCM for their own account, but only *because* the returns were thought to be risk-free. Therefore once the Wall Street banks started getting in on the action LTCM had to find pastures new, and this was where it all went wrong.

The partners had by this time become convinced of their own genius and had fallen victim to 'groupthink.' They thought that they could merely use the same arbitrage techniques in different markets. Furthermore by this time the investment capital controlled by LTCM was huge. The law of large numbers dictates that as the sum invested increases it becomes harder and harder to find viable investment opportunities.[11]

Unfortunately for LTCM there were few if any investment opportunities for capital on such large scale. The opportunities that they identified quickly moved away from the traditional risk-free arbitrage that LTCM was designed to employ and more towards the rampant speculation that the investors in the fund sought refuge from. The most important criterion for many of LTCM's investors was not capital appreciation but capital preservation. Using the theory that you only need to get rich once, the majority of the LTCM investors were looking for capital preservation with a rate of return in excess of the rate available from bank deposits. It is this requirement that hedge fund managers purport to be able to achieve.[12]

So once the opportunities had dried up, it all began to fall apart for LTCM. The 'chaos' was created by the fact that the partners' deluded sense of their own self-importance and expertise had now gone through

---

11.   Warren Buffett has had this problem for years. His strategy of buying equity stakes in good companies has evolved into the need to buy the whole company if the amount invested is going to make any difference to the return generated by Berkshire Hathaway.
12.   This is also why many hedge funds do not stay around for very long.

the roof. The banks that had been quite happy to lend enormous sums to LTCM were now competing with the hedge fund. The markets upon which LTCM initially fed had dried up. Most importantly, the luck with which they had started 1994 with had now deserted them. If David Mullins *had* convinced the Federal Reserve Chairman of the need for a steep rise in interest rates in February 1994 before leaving for LTCM, he obviously no longer had the opportunity to do so again.

Therefore if LTCM were *really* concerned with long-term capital management they would at this point have returned the cash to their investors. Unfortunately this would have necessitated unwinding the massive derivative positions that LTCM had built up. This however was impossible because there was no other institution upon which to unload the positions. LTCM had sought to be the biggest and the best but in so doing they had become too big a fish for the pond that supported it and very, very soon LTCM found itself to be the food on which the other fish were to feast.

By not returning the cash to investors LTCM instead merely fuelled investors' appetite for more 'risk-free' excess returns. On and on it went, the never-ending search for the Holy Grail. The search took LTCM to Italian bonds, through Asian bonds until the hedge fund finally settled in Russia. Russia of all places, the once bastion of communism was now being turned into a model of unfettered capitalism. The classic LTCM strategy of playing the convergence of bond yields would be put to work in Russia. Russia, the once sworn enemy of the West and the United States in particular, was now home to the largest hedge fund in the world. Furthermore, by this time the success of LTCM had spawned so many imitators that the whole hedge fund community was following suit and was seeking to exploit opportunities in Russia. That the bond yields on Russian securities were wide was a fact. Unfortunately they were wide for a very good reason. Russia was not a good investment. Russia was in fact outright speculation. The hedge fund community was speculating that once converted to capitalism Russia would move along the path without a blip. The bet was that Russia would quickly embrace the Anglo-American model of capitalism and in so doing would provide easy pickings for yield conversion. The bet was basically that the spread between Russian bonds and US Treasuries would contract because the LTCM economic models dictated that they were too wide. This is how the United States financial system almost imploded in 1998. It nearly imploded because a few 'rock and rollers' in Greenwich, bankrolled by a few 'rock and rollers' on Wall Street, thought that they could re-write social and geo-political history in a few years for the sole purpose of lining their own pockets with the benefits derived from other people's money. Well, of course, it did not work.

As the contagion that had engulfed Asia spread to Russia, the Russian government defaulted on their debt. United States Treasury bills are seen as the benchmark of investment security *only* because the United States government is seen as extremely unlikely to default on its debt. The government bonds of all countries are judged *solely* on their likelihood of default. Russian government bonds were cheap exactly *because* there was a real likelihood that the Russian government would default on their debt. Unfortunately for the United States financial system, the 'rock and rollers' at the heart of the system had collectively lost their minds. They had totally lost the plot. 'Gekko' greed and hyper-competition had led to a 'group-think' induced inability to see the wood for the trees. It was not about money for the LTCM partners at this point. Especially for John Meriwether, it had always been about proving a point. It was about proving that they were the best, that they were better than the rest because they were *smarter* than they rest. That they were smart was true. The academic achievements of the option-pricing professors proved it. Unfortunately the protagonists at LTCM were still human, and human beings are really not that smart at all. Nature rules. The human condition also rules. The creation of LTCM was a 'chaos' theorist's dream. The strategy of LTCM had within it the seeds of its own 'chaotic' destruction, but only after a period of staggering chaos-free success.

The lessons learnt from Long Term Capital Management

There are important lessons to be leant from the LTCM debacle. However it is only the lessons regarding bank lending that we need to concern ourselves with here. For it is only the excessive and over-aggressive lending by the Wall Street investment banks that enabled LTCM to grow into such a monster of a hedge fund that threatened to destroy the United States banking system.

- Economics must take into account human nature and the unpredictability of human nature.

- Arbitrage is low risk and generates low profits.

- Investment banks lend huge sums to unregulated hedge funds. These loans are often placed off the balance sheet.

- Derivatives are dangerous to both the party and the counter party.

- Share options encourage excessive risk-taking.

- Excessive secrecy is dangerous. LTCM did not disclose details of its trading but the banks did not care.

- Buffett says *"don't invest if you cannot understand it."*

- Market risks are more correlated than many economic models allow for.

'Rock and roll economics' recognizes the potential for even the most sober economic participant to lose the plot and to turn into a 'rock and roller.' We are all human and life is richer and more interesting for that fact. However in order to complete our understanding of 'rock and roll economics' we must go head to head with one of the biggest 'rock and rollers' around. In the next chapter we go into battle with none other than Mr. George Soros.

7

The Hypocrisy of Modern Finance

We will now examine the work of George Soros in which he looks at the Asian financial crisis of 1998 and analyses the crucial point now reached in the history of Anglo-American capitalism.[1] This chapter will investigate the role played by morally deficient participants in the financial system who are responsible for creating havoc for their own personal pleasure and profit whilst espousing theories and solutions to the problems of the world economy.

George Soros is the financier who gained the notorious reputation as the man who broke the Bank of England. His part in the United Kingdom currency devaluation of 1992 sealed his reputation as a legend within the hedge fund industry.[2]

This chapter is called "The Hypocrisy of Modern Finance" because the Anglo-American society is built on hypocrisy. From the Native American saying that *"white man speak with forked tongue"* to President Clinton's infamous *"I did not have sexual relations with that woman, Miss Lewinsky"*, it is a history of hypocrisy. It is a history of callously claiming the moral high ground whilst demonizing those who struggle to

1. *"The Crisis in Global Capitalism"*
2. George Soros runs Soros Fund Management, the principle investment advisor to Quantum Fund, a Curacao-based investment firm. Quantum Fund is generally recognized as having the best performance records of any investment fund in the world during its 26-year history.

cope with the consequences of the actions of the high and mighty. It is as if hypocrisy is a code to which the leaders and would-be leaders subscribe and promise to uphold. One may even call it a "Hypocritic Oath" as it seems to have the permanence and reverence of the Hippocratic oath to which medical practitioners must subscribe.

In his book published in the wake of the 1998 Russian financial crisis and the Long Term Capital Management hedge fund implosion, Soros talks about the need for a global political system to manage and oversee the global capitalist system that embraces the developed and developing countries of the world. He argues that without such a political system the global capitalist system is in danger of breaking down. He further argues that it is the excesses of capitalism that pose the greatest threat.

The global capitalist system of which he speaks is essentially an Anglo-American model of capitalism that has been exported to the rest of the world by a form of creeping ideological imperialism. Since the 1980s when the flow of capital across borders was removed, investment capital has been free to be held in offshore tax havens and to move to countries that provide the best investment opportunities. Unfortunately this liberalization of investment capital flows had a side effect of allowing the same freedom to investment capital that is essentially short-term in nature. This global short-term speculative capital is the source of the global instability of which Soros writes. Paradoxically, Soros himself is, or at least was, one of the biggest players in this field. His writings therefore need to be taken critically. His previous books yielded a philosophy that reveals a barely concealed desire to impose his version of a fair society on the rest of the world.[3] He calls his ideal 'open society' but it seems at best naively individualistic and at worst brazenly fascist.

---

3.   *"Alchemy of Finance"* and *"Soros on Soros"*

Soros openly admits that hedge funds like his Quantum fund are more likely to be actively involved in changing a trend in financial markets once a trend becomes unsustainable. By way of justification he claims that this is as a result of a focus on absolute returns rather than relative returns.[4] The clients of a hedge fund will not tolerate negative returns on the basis that the returns are less negative than the relevant index or less negative than other investment funds.

It is further claimed by way of justification that it is more advantageous for any unsustainable trend in financial markets to be reversed sooner rather than later. Unfortunately this is Soros's personal opinion based upon an acceptance of the moral superiority of the profit motive. It is certainly financially beneficial for some participants to capitalize on the reversal of an unsustainable trend at the expense of late arriving trend followers. However it does not necessarily follow that a sudden reversal of the prevailing trend is beneficial for the citizens of the respective country or for the market as a whole. It may well be more beneficial to let the trend continue to boom and to eventually bust of its own accord. In one example Soros states that at the outbreak of the Asian crisis 50% of the world's cranes were operating in Shanghai.[5] This is the kind of statistic that puts boom time madness into perspective. Once information such as this becomes well known it starts to trigger a reversal of trend because even a layman will be able to see that the trend is unsustainable. However, the ongoing property development in Shanghai assumed that the prevailing trend would continue. Unfortunately as the boom/bust sequence continued it became increasingly clear that the property developers who had not completed their projects would be unlikely to achieve the expected returns. It is at this point that busts accelerate.

---

4. The goal of absolute returns entails achieving a positive return on investment rather than losing less money than one's peers or the relevant market index.
5. *"The Crisis in Global Capitalism"*, p50

The previous analysis of the Russian financial crisis shows that it was the devaluation of the Russian ruble that triggered the wholesale dumping of Russian securities that in turn caused Long Term Capital Management (LTCM) to implode. Currency devaluations would not normally endanger the global capitalist system. It only did so on this occasion because LTCM was highly leveraged in derivative transactions that did not fully take into account the possibility of default by the Russian government. It was because of the risk of default that the securities concerned were priced so low.[6] The credit risk differential between Russian bonds and United States treasuries would not realistically narrow in a short period of time. Any rational observer would have concluded at the time that it would take many decades before the Russian financial system would command anywhere near the same kind of respect as that commanded by the United States and other Western governments. Therefore it should have been expected that the yield differential would remain relatively wide for the foreseeable future.

Furthermore, leverage in the financial system as a result of the growth of derivative products threatens to detonate the whole financial system as it has previously detonated individual institutions.[7] Profits on derivative transactions can only be made at the expense of the party on the other side of the trade. Therefore if the counter-party defaults, the profits are not realized. It would only take one large default along the lines of LTCM to increase the risks of counter-party default to such an extent that institutions would call in their derivative trades triggering unexpected losses for the counter-parties.[8] These participants such as Soros and his Quantum fund may well be well-meaning but ill-informed players in a game that they have no part in shaping, or they may well be vacuous hypocrites seeking to shift the blame for the prob-

6. Low priced bonds have a correspondingly high yield.
7. See Barings Bank in 1995, Orange County and other United States Savings & Loan institutions in the early 1990s.
8. *"The Crisis in Global Capitalism"*, p170

lems in the world from their own doorstep as they seek to prolong the game from which they derive so much pleasure and profit.

The basis of Soros' argument is that a global political system is necessary because of the instability of the global capitalist system. However there is not really a global capitalist system in this sense. Investment capital may flow internationally but markets are still national and governed by national regulators. The talk is still of a UK market, a US market and a Japanese market. Investors in one country may be free to invest in another country if they are willing to take on the currency and geopolitical risk, but the recipient market is still national in nature.

The major thrust of Soros's work is that some of the basic laws of economics that today drive understanding and policy constitute a fatally flawed, and over-simplified version of reality. Soros' viewpoint is that economic theory fails to take into account the human element in economic decision-making and hence leads to predictions that are unlikely to be accurate, and outcomes that are therefore unpredictable. These unpredictable outcomes are in turn likely to create opportunities for further policy errors in the future.

Standard economic theory states that markets tend towards equilibrium but Soros contends that markets tend to overshoot and often go from one extreme to another. Taken at face value, this is not a remarkable statement and the propensity of markets to go from boom to bust is quite clear to even the passing observer. However, it is Soros's contention that this predilection should be factored into economic theory and not merely dismissed as an aberration whenever a boom/bust episode occurs. He contends that financial markets actively create the future that they predict in a two-way connection that he calls 'reflexivity'.

Unfortunately what Soros fails to accept is that economic theory is a necessary simplification for the aid of students of economics and that the theory is a means to control human actions and not merely to reflect it. The excesses of capitalism that he alludes to and seeks to model are the exact same excesses that the modern central banks are seeking to control. Furthermore, the criticism of the tendency towards equilibrium is unjust because although financial markets may not actually *reach* equilibrium they still *tend* towards equilibrium in that they swing backwards and forwards past the point of equilibrium. If a swing is very excessive in one direction it seeks only to ensure that the bust that follows the boom will be quite severe in the other direction. These market swings may continue for a long time but the point of equilibrium acts as a marker that should remind participants how far the pendulum must swing back in order to redress a mis-pricing episode.

Soros further claims that economic experts will tend to respond to a developing boom in asset prices by claiming that prices will revert to equilibrium after which they will continue to move according to the previous levels of supply and demand. Soros says that this is not necessarily so, and that the boom may continue for a much longer time before the eventual bust ensues. Hedge funds such as Quantum therefore often seek to push the boom further in the same direction because this is the easy way to profits. The bust is usually prompted by a discovery by the participants of the fatal flaw in the argument behind the level of prices. What Soros fails to acknowledge is that his theory of reflexivity is in itself reflexive in so far as other participants imitated his methods. As they did so the success of the method initially increased. This acted to validate the method and further increased its popularity. As more and more participants sought to push booms further and further whilst at the same time being fully aware of the flaws in the investment thesis, the instability of the capitalist system increased. It is this instability that is leading to larger and larger booms and busts. The fact that the participants are seeking to maximize their profits before exiting the market before everyone realizes the flaws almost guarantee a bust at the end of the boom. In this way modern financial markets have become to resemble the game of 'chicken' in classic game theory.[9]

The solution to the crisis in global capitalism proposed by Soros is the creation of 'open society' that encompasses institutions with built in error-correcting mechanisms. Unfortunately for Soros, what he calls 'open society' is in fact already in existence. It is 'open society' as opposed to the 'closed society' of the fascists. It is 'open society' that is the dominant form of society in the Western world at this time. The rules that govern society are modified through the democratic election system. Unfortunately the system has been corrupted by the same capitalism that the system is supposed to control. Representative democracy has gone from "*one person, one vote*" to "*one dollar, one vote*" because politicians are open to corrosive influence in the guise of fundraising donations.

The international political government that Soros claims is missing is already in existence in the form of the United Nations (UN), the World Trade Organization (WTO), the International Monetary Fund (IMF), and other institutions such as the central banks of the G7 countries. It is quite often said that it is the role of central banks and the other institutions in charge of economic welfare is to take away the punch bowl when the party has become out of control. This entails sober people sitting in judgement upon the actions of the citizens that make up society and determining when they as a whole have had enough. However this power is quite obviously open to abuse. It can be argued that the initial success of the Long Term Capital Management hedge fund that imploded in 1998 was as a result of the former Federal Reserve vice-chairman's influence on policy as he left office to become a partner in the fund. David W. Mullins used his influence to

---

9. Two cars speed towards each other in a potential head-on crash situation. One wins by not swerving before the other player. However if no player swerves both players obviously lose. Psychopaths are best at this game but only against non-psychopaths. Two psychopaths will just kill themselves. It has been said that the best tactic is to throw the steering wheel out of the window so that the other player knows that one cannot turn and therefore must swerve to save his or her life. This tactic is extreme but effective.

persuade the Federal Reserve chairman that the economy and the bond market in particular were over-heating and in need of a dose of higher interest rates. When the Federal Funds rate was suddenly increased without warning, it caused a sharp correction in the financial markets. The fact that LTCM was able to profit from the distress caused to the other market participants at the time could be put down to coincidence by more generous commentators; but there is a case to answer regarding the quite glaring conflict of interest that lay behind the advice of the vice-chairman.[10]

The fact that the Anglo Saxon capitalist system is deeply flawed and is in imminent danger of collapse is the paradox and the hypocrisy behind modern finance and modern society. The concept of 'rock and roll economics' that is proposed in this book is an alternative to the current sociological and economic organization and is a more acceptable and understandable alternative than 'open society'. 'Open society' is an ideology in the same way that fascism and socialism were ideologies. They were flawed because they proposed to supply the one and final answer to the problems of the organization of human existence. They sought to provide wealth, prosperity, and ultimate happiness to all citizens based upon the writings of a few intellectual elites whose ivory-tower credentials were patchy to say the least.

'Rock and roll economics' on the other hand, proposes that society, rather than dictating to the majority the wishes of the minority, seeks to allow citizens to form their own views and to express them in their own way. It is an ethos of doing what one wants to do even if it is wrong. Any negative outcome does not need to be seen as a mistake or an unintended consequence; instead, it is seen as a desirable outcome of human choice.

---

10. *"When Genius Failed"*, pp36–41

The concept of 'open society' requires an agreement on what is right and wrong and proposes that citizens must be ready to do what is right even if it has unpleasant consequences. However 'rock and roll economics' reflects that these values are not set in stone and can be changed at will. Citizens are free and they can choose to be good, or they can choose to be bad, or they can be any combination of both as they see fit. The point is that there is no right and there is no wrong. People are complex human beings and there is no sense in trying to deny it.

Soros goes on to contrast the present version of global capitalism with the system based on the gold standard. The absence today of shared beliefs and ethical standards is highlighted as one of the major differences between the two periods. It is then claimed that presently, fundamental principles must originate internally because there is no external authority in the modern world. It is argued that religion and science were previously exalted external authorities but they have become increasingly open to question and therefore cannot be relied upon.

Unfortunately Soros does not recognize that these external authorities have always come under scrutiny throughout history and were constantly questioned even during the height of their popularity. To claim that these challenges have made the authorities redundant is premature at best. The claim appears mainly to be a convenient justification for a rejection of religious and scientific values to be replaced by the arbitrary will of individuals seeking to dominate other members of society. This is very similar to the theories proposed by Nietzsche that were adopted and adapted to such devastating effect by the European fascists in the 1930s.[11]

For society to function well it needs to develop in a similar way to the way in which modern computer software is developed. The concept of

---

11. "*Thus Spake Zarathustra*", Friedrich Nietzsche, 1883–92. Nietzsche was permanently insane from 1889.

'versioning' whereby software is never actually finished but evolves over several 'versions' to meet the customer's needs has proved very successful. The concept accepts the fact that the first version at least, if not the first few versions, will only provide some of the benefits that will be ultimately desired by the customer.[12] However 'versioning' is successful because the profits from the sales from one version are ploughed back into research and development for the next version. This next version is released very soon after the previous version. The cycle of versions is very rapid and keeps the customer relatively satisfied whilst not allowing competitors to catch up.[13] In order for these techniques to be successful there must be a commitment to continuous improvement by society as society must, by definition, be willing to accept imperfections at any point in time. Society will be able to tolerate this because there is a built-in assurance that any 'bugs' will be corrected in the next version.[14]

'Rock and roll economics' is not the same as the theory proposed by the proponents of laissez-faire economics. These economists claim that society benefits from citizens expressing their will through their choices in the marketplace. They urge people to be selfish and individualistic, to think only of oneself and not to worry about the consequences. The philosophy is summed up by Margaret Thatcher's famous quote that "*There is no such thing as Society. There are individual men and women, and there are families.*"[15] The problem with this claim is that the philosophy behind it is essentially anti-social. The actions that it promotes engenders within citizens the same characteristics that are present in

---

12. See the history of Microsoft as told by James Wallace & Jim Erickson in "*Hard Drive*"

13. This cycle of incremental improvements is similar to the Japanese manufacturing technique of 'kaisen' that proved so successful in that country's rise from post-Second World War devastation to global economic dominance by the end of the 1980s.

14. Errors in computer software are referred to as 'bugs' after a live insect crawled into the circuitry of one of the earliest computers causing a software error.

15. "*Women's Own*" 31 October 1987

people with anti-social personal disorder. These are the same people who were once termed psychopaths.[16] It is quite clear that the post-1980s selfish attitudes exported from the United States as part of that country's cultural imperialism is a very subtle form of fascism and is extremely dangerous to the proper functioning of a modern democracy.[17] Soros also claims that the doubts about the relevance of previous religious and scientific values has effectively created a vacuum that has allowed the relative certainty granted by monetary values to gain the upper hand. It is widely acknowledged that the United States has always held the achievement of wealth and success as the ultimate driving force for its citizens. The fact the early settlers in the country combined these beliefs with a strong belief in religious values is part of the paradox that makes the United States such a unique nation. The brazenly materialistic attitude prevalent in the United States can be contrasted to the values still prominent in what Adam Smith called "*the mother country.*" In the United Kingdom the class system operates to hinder progress beyond class boundaries. It is not sufficient for monetary wealth to allow access to certain privileged positions in society. In the UK one must be "*of the right sort*" and despite claims of the merits of 'classlessness' it is still widely accepted that there are benefits to society as a whole of a well-established class hierarchy.

'Rock and roll economics' can be applied to the history of capitalism in the same way as Soros tries to apply 'reflexivity' to it. In this way it can be seen that capitalism was 'rocking' after it emerged victorious in the long war against communism. There was no alternative to the laissez-faire, unfettered capitalism that spread from the Anglo-American countries to encompass the major developed countries in the world. Now that capitalism has been unable to contain its own excesses and has started 'rolling', it can arguably be seen as a positive development. The fact that this process is uncontrollable is the essence of 'rock and

---

16. Refer to the Oxford Dictionary of Psychology.
17. "*Liar's Poker*" by Michael Lewis.

roll economics.' It is very unlikely that the process will end at an equilibrium state but will 'roll' too far in the other direction. However, it is the very peripatetic nature of the 'rock and roll economics' process that gives it its legitimacy. If the laissez-faire movement was based on Adam Smith's assertion that all government intervention tends to make matters worse, the best course of action must therefore be to let the 'rock and roll' process evolve according to the wishes of the citizens who make up the societies concerned.[18]

No government or society that purports to be free can seriously expect to protect citizens from making bad decisions. This is because the ability to make a bad decision is at the heart of personal freedom. The fact that many things in life that are pleasurable are also harmful is unfortunately a fact of life. From cigarettes and alcohol, to fast cars and fast women, life is full of temptations and diversions that court danger with each indulgence. To seek to protect people from over-indulgence in these areas is to remove a safety valve in the human condition the lack of which may have unintended consequences. 'Rock and roll economics' accepts and allows for the ability of citizens as people and consumers to make choices that they knowingly will regret at a later date. From over-spending to over-eating, freedom is about getting it wrong occasionally. The choice of buying those expensive shoes that never did quite fit and subsequently remain untouched in the wardrobe for years is a choice that is as economically valid as a similar purchase of a pair of sensible shoes that are worn all the time. The ability for an entrepreneur to over-expand his business for personal power and prestige before it implodes in an avalanche of bad debts and unwanted product is part of human nature. As a result of this aspect of human nature, society as a whole will not be able to progress to its full capabilities until the straightjacket of pomposity disguised as superior knowledge of what is acceptable and what is not acceptable is finally removed. Not

---

18. *"The Wealth of Nations"*

every teenager who dabbles in illegal substances becomes a drug addict. Some even go on to become Presidents and Prime Ministers.

This does not that mean that society should encourage illegal, anti-social, or immoral activity. Rather it accepts that the definitions of which actions are acceptable and which actions are not acceptable is a judgement that is not consistent with the claim of being a free society. Even societies based on strong religious values hold within them the seeds of their own destruction. In these societies people who do not share the values will obviously find the society oppressive and intolerable.[19]

The core concepts that Soros re-introduces in *The Crisis Of Global Capitalism* are the concepts of 'fallibility' and 'reflexivity'. These concepts underpin the understanding of the current collapse of the Anglo-American capitalist system. The concept of 'fallibility' is basically the idea that economic, political and social life incorporates the decisions of thinking participants and that these participants are fallible in their reasoning. They are therefore likely on occasion to produce results that would not occur according to standard economic theory. The concept of 'reflexivity' is the idea that the thinking of the participants directly influences the outcome of the events in which the participants are participating. The thinking of the participants is simultaneously affected by the expected outcome. The result is a feedback mechanism of price and price expectation, a blur between participant perception and reality that Soros calls 'reflexivity'. However for a situation to be truly reflexive it must be accompanied by imperfect understanding. Obviously if the answer could be known, or the correct price determined, there could not be an evolution of a boom/bust scenario. The old maxim that for every buyer there must be a seller holds true in so far as if the correct price could be known it would not be advantageous for

---

19. For example the Taliban regime in Afghanistan was seen as oppressive and roused little support against the US-led 'war on terror' in late 2001.

anyone to pay a higher price than the product or security is worth. Imperfect understanding is the key to reflexive activity in so far as neither buyer nor seller can be totally sure that the price at which they have struck their bargain is in fact the fair and reasonable price. In then follows that it would be extremely advantageous for any potential buyer or seller to be able to determine the correct price. In these situations it follows that there will be a continuous price determination process evolving in a vacuum of uncertainty brought about by the absence of perfect understanding. As the boom/bust scenario unfolds, it is this vacuum that sucks in more and more buyers and sellers.

The reflexive process is more often than not self-correcting rather than self-reinforcing. An all out boom/bust sequence is altogether much more rare and tends to manifest itself once per generation in any financial or social sphere. Unfortunately there will always be boom/bust sequences because the participants are human. It will not happen very often but the potential always remains. Central banks are on constant alert for inflation and have official and unofficial targets to adhere to. It may be argued that in addition to this crucial role they should also be on the look out for potential boom/bust sequences. It appears that the fact that not all potential boom/bust sequences unfold to their full potential has encouraged the authorities to ignore them in the hope that any undeveloped boom/bust sequence will pass them by. This 'head in the sand' approach is dangerous and has contributed to the reflexive nature of reflexivity as the notoriety of the hedge funds that use this approach has encouraged more and more imitators.

The current UK housing market is a classic example of rampant asset price inflation caused by a reflexive boom/bust sequence. The fact that the stock of residential property in the UK is referred to as a market at all reveals the perception that houses are to be bought and sold rather to be one's main residence. Residential property is treated like a market and constantly referred to as a market to the extent that price indices are published every month by the two biggest mortgage lenders.[20] This conversion of housing stock into a market that holds a high proportion of many citizens' net wealth has meant that any tendency towards boom and bust has a high impact on the UK economy. For the Bank of England (BoE) to treat the housing market as an aside to the other monetary measures and economic indicators surely amounts to a dereliction of duty. The need for stability in the price of UK housing stock in order to stop a repeat of the 1980s boom and bust should be just as important in the mind of the Bank of England as the control of inflation.

Unfortunately this has not been the case as a similar boom has been allowed to develop during the 2000–2003 period. Once again rising house prices has led to more borrowing by consumers in the form of equity loans. This borrowing is only made possible by the same lending that inflates house prices. If the banks and building societies did not lend so aggressively there would be no price rise and no subsequent equity loan. At the height of a housing boom, it is more advantageous for individuals to build houses rather than borrowing to buy. To profit by buying a house using a mortgage assumes continued borrowing by other participants in the market. The phenomenon of rising house prices is merely an example of asset price inflation. By way of contrast, the profit margin available by building a house is due to the effort and risk involved. It is economically justifiable according to Adam Smith as he claims that productivity is the only way to wealth.[21]

Many commentators are currently predicting that the boom will end soon and the market will return to price rises in line with average earnings and growth in the overall economy. Unfortunately according to reflexivity theory this will not happen. It appears that UK house prices are moving into 'far from equilibrium' territory as the declared need to dampen down the housing market using higher interest rates is caught

---

20. Nationwide and Halifax produce monthly indices of average house prices with year-on-year price movements and predictions for the near future.

21. *"Wealth of Nations"*

in the vice between the need to close the interest rate gap with continental Europe before Britain can join the Euro, and the need to lower interest rates to prevent the world economy slipping into a double-dip recession after the late 1990s credit-fuelled over-investment boom.[22] It can be argued that BoE policy should embrace wider methods of controlling asset prices rather than merely relying on the blunt instrument of interest rates. It is quite conceivable, and not wholly undesirable, that the BoE could restrain mortgage lenders in some way as an unsustainable boom develops. One example would be to make compulsory the adherence to the voluntary code prescribed by the Council of Mortgage Lenders (CML). This organization comprises the largest and most influential mortgage lenders but does not compel its members to stick to pre-determined lending criteria. In normal times this conduct is satisfactory. However during boom times when the mortgage lenders have begun to lend recklessly and aggressively, it needs the BoE to be able to prevent the mortgage lenders enticing consumers into a debt trap. It is this debt trap that some consumers will fall prey to whilst others will profit from the leverage offered by mortgage lending of upwards of 90% of the property value.[23] The long-term trend of maximum mortgage value as a multiple of earnings has been stable at three times earnings during the last thirty years. However in some recently reported cases this multiple has been allowed to increase to five, six, or seven times earnings. This is especially true in London and the South East where property prices are rising fastest and threatening to move beyond the reach of many first-time buyers. If the BoE were able to enforce maximum mortgages as a percentage of property value and/or as a multiple of earnings, the growth in lending will be able to be controlled and the result would be greater stability in the level of house

---

22. As of March 2003 the gap between UK short-term rates and Euro rates is 150 basis points or 1.50%
23. Some mortgage companies are lending in excess of the property value and in some cases up to 125% to first-time buyers struggling to get on the housing ladder and to furnish their homes.

prices and the reduction in the likelihood of a boom/bust sequence occurring.

Yet another near perfect example of a reflexive boom/bust sequence was the dot-com mania in the late 1990s. Rising share prices not only influenced the fundamentals but towards the end of the boom they *became* the fundamentals. Companies such as Worldcom and Enron were organized with the primary goal of increasing the share price. The products and service that were on offer were merely a means to an end. In many cases there was no business behind the company. It was pure fraud. Some newly formed companies were merely put together to fleece investors who had bought into the hype because of the rising stock prices. To the extent that the frauds were pre-meditated attempts to deceive investors, and that the companies were arranged with that purpose in mind, it is clear that many examples of dot-com businesses were merely examples of organized crime.

The mania seemed irrational at the time to many observers, and is even more irrational in hindsight. It is however perfectly understandable using the light of 'rock and roll economics.' Due to the trend-following nature of the financial markets it was possible to amass a small fortune by riding the boom in dot-com share prices. This is because it is only at the turning points in a boom/bust sequence that investors who have mis-timed their climb onto the bandwagon will get hurt. As the share price of the companies began to cease to be reflected in the fundamentals, investors turned increasingly to 'technical analysis' as a way of understanding and predicting the movements of share prices.[24] The simple beauty of technical analysis is that it relies on other investors doing the fundamental analysis that moves the share prices. The popularity of technical analysis itself became reflexive as less and less people

---

24. The technical investor merely analyses the share price movements seeking to identify and exploit any prevailing trend.

bothered with the fundamentals. When the turning point came, the prevailing technical trend reversed and share prices crashed.

In contrast to the snugness of 'rock and roll economics,' the fit is not so tight when the theory of 'reflexivity' is overlaid on social and political history such as the history of capitalism. The major problem area is the concept of 'fallibility'. Now that people have accepted capitalism as *the* economic system of choice at the expense of any other alternative, it is obvious that 'fallibility' is absent. The absence of fallibility in financial markets increases the likelihood that the phenomenon under observation will reach 'far from equilibrium' levels. To allow for the concept of 'fallibility' is to accept that the decision-maker may be wrong. Unfortunately this is very hard for the majority of people to do. The fact that Soros has been able to make out-sized returns in the financial markets because of this unique ability is testament to the fact that it is very difficult. The reason for this is that the education system promotes the idea of right and wrong answers and pupils are graded accordingly. Therefore it is extremely difficult for a person having completed his or her education to be able to adopt the attitude that it is acceptable to be wrong when coming to a decision. Even if a person were able to do this, he or she may find that society as a whole does not accept such a seemingly blasé attitude about important decisions and may rightly suggest that such an individual is not qualified for the position, thus making his or her job untenable.

Furthermore, economics, as with other social science disciplines, has stolen some of the kudos belonging to the pure scientists by seeking to arrive at truths that will sit alongside scientific discoveries such as the laws of gravity. Unfortunately the unpredictability of human nature renders such pursuits futile because the social scientific 'laws' will constantly change. Social science can only hope to seek to understand a phenomenon, as it exists at the time of enquiry. How long any phenomenon will last is entirely a matter for the individuals under observation; therefore, any 'law' of social science must come with the caveat that it has built-in obsolescence. Some of the social sciences—and this is especially true of economics—are not about the pursuit of truth. The aim of much of social science theory is to seek ways of controlling the population under observation. The claim of scientific truth, and the status that goes with it, only makes it easier to make people believe and to crush any dissent. Such false claims are, however, crucial to the success of the social scientists as the population will have no reason to comply with rules that are obviously the whim of an ivory-tower specialist in a discipline that may well be nothing more than smoke and mirrors.

Contrary to Soros's assertion, modern Western society does have the ability to improve itself. However the power to make those improvements is restricted to those qualified to do so. One high profile example is the proposal to remove the double-jeopardy law in the UK after the collapse of the Stephen Lawrence murder trial.[25] The failure of the trial enabled the five defendants to walk free, safe in the knowledge that they could not be brought to court again for a murder that the evidence suggests the defendants did in fact commit. This ability to change the rules of society from within promotes the status quo but allows changes in society to occur but only after great deliberation.

In the chapter "*The Global Capitalist System*", Soros states that:

> "*If the global capitalist survives the present period of testing, this period will be followed by a period of further acceleration that will carry the system into far-from-equilibrium territory if it is not there already.*"

Soros claimed that the disintegration of capitalism had already begun, but contradicted his own words on more than one occasion. In fact, after the financial markets recovered due to central bank intervention, Soros withdrew the opinion in later interviews.[26] It can be argued that the excesses of late 1999–2000 were the occurrence of this move into

---

25. The law of double jeopardy is the law that prevents a defendant being tried twice for the same crime.

'far-from-equilibrium' territory. It may be seen to represent the final blow-off in the domination of Anglo-American capitalism. The stock market correction that began in March 2000 and continued through into 2001, 2002, and 2003 may be seen to be the start of the decline of Anglo-American capitalism. The attack on the World Trade Centre on September 11 2001 may look to the observer to be an unrelated coincidence, but it is usual for a boom/bust sequence to begin to unravel by itself without external provocation before being hit by an unexpected occurrence that reinforces the change in trend and provides a wake-up call for any participants still expecting a return to the good old days.[27]

The unease between religious fundamentalists and what Soros calls 'market fundamentalists' was highlighted in his work, but because of a previous rejection of the importance of religious values, the importance of the conflict was not recognized. It was envisaged that the two sides would be able to work together towards the goal of 'open society.' Unfortunately there was a failure to appreciate just how seriously the religious fundamentalists take their religions. The events of September 11 2001 were a wake-up call for those who thought that 'market fundamentalism' would be able to sweep all before it without much of a fight. Now that this fight has begun and the United States is responding with the self-declared 'War on Terror,' it is unlikely that the 'religious fundamentalists' will survive as a political force. Unfortunately the views of these citizens will not be changed by military force. As Shakespeare wrote in *Richard II*, "lions may make leopards tame…but not change his spots."

---

26. In an interview with the Financial Times in early 2000, he claimed that he was wrong which is understandable given his embracing of the concept of fallibility. It is possible however to be doubly fallible and to claim to have been wrong when one is actually correct albeit it a little premature.
27. An observer remarked at the time that the way the twin towers fell was akin to a mirror image of the Apollo rocket launch and represented the end of the era of US global dominance that began with the Apollo launch in 1969.

Although the capitalist system survived the Russian collapse in 1998, the Nasdaq inspired crash of March 2000 marked what Soros calls the 'moment of truth' and it has been downhill ever since. We have now passed the 'crossover point' and are heading downwards. The United States stock markets have fallen into a vicious cycle after three successive years of negative returns. Mutual fund redemptions have led to falls in the stock markets that in turn have led to more mutual fund redemptions. In the United States stock market, technical analysis of the S&P500 index points to a further 40% fall from 930 to 550 that will take prices well below fair value.[28] This will lead to lower interest rates in order to stimulate the economy and interest rates could quite possibly continue the steady fall towards zero as they have already done in Japan.[29] If US interest rates fall to near zero, it will finally mark the confirmation of the deflationary environment that central banks dread, but an environment that many business leaders have been living with for years.[30] This realization will be painful for any individual or organization that has not prepared for it.

One painful example is the fact that many company final salary pension schemes are being wound up because of the realization that in a low inflation to near deflationary environment, the pension funds will not be able to generate the investment returns needed to pay the pensions of the retired employees. This second vicious cycle has developed because the pension funds of the largest companies in the UK have shortfalls that will need to be topped-up by the parent company. The top-up will need to come from the business itself in one way or another and will therefore affect the annual profits and earnings per share. This fall in profits will in turn affect the price/earnings (PE) ratio of the

---

28. This analysis is valid at the time of writing being May 2003.
29. United States interest rates are still currently at 1.25% whilst interest rates in Japan have been stuck at near zero for years with no sign of a turnaround in the economy.
30. The British Retail Consortium publishes prices for retail sales and these have shown falling prices on a year-on-year basis for several years.

company and make it a less attractive investment. This increase in the PE ratio will be met by selling from investment funds as they seek to re-price the investment. In a relatively efficient market, this re-pricing mechanism will work quite quickly and the falling share prices of the largest UK companies will depress the FTSE100 index and that will in turn reduce the returns from the pension funds of those same companies. This cycle will only end once the share prices of the companies concerned have fallen so low as to present bargain opportunities to investors other than the pension funds and investment funds that are already fully committed to equities.[31]

The financial sector will of course be the most affected sector and the re-rating of the shares of banks and finance companies has already started. In the United Kingdom stock market, the dividend yield on many banks is greater than the rate of deposit. It is therefore more advantageous to buy the shares of the banks than to leave the money on deposit. Of course this advantage only holds as long as the share price does not fall by enough to offset the difference in return. The current market pricing mechanism obviously assumes that this is the case and is therefore pricing in a swing past the point of equilibrium and to a classic boom/bust reversal of the previous trend. This previous trend saw banking shares become the prominent component of the FTSE100 index in late 1998.

Finally, Soros asserted that the final crisis of capitalism would be political in nature as indigenous movements seek to recapture national wealth from the multi-national corporations. However the crisis appears to be legal as the investors who were defrauded during the technology bubble of 1998–2001 launch legal claims against the investment banks and other institutions that were responsible. The legion of disgruntled investors is now a powerful new class that has

---

31. Only investors such as Warren Buffett would be able to profit from the depression-level share prices because he had steadfastly refused to buy over-valued securities and stocks of 'new economy' technology companies.

already begun to re-write the rules of Wall Street and may indeed have begun to re-write the rules of capitalism itself.

8

In Search Of Nirvana

The crowd outside was a mass of black and white. They were shouting in unison. "We're the barmy Geordie army, la-la-la, la-la." The chanting went on for several minutes but they would not be silenced. Fathers had come with their sons, uncles with their nephews. They had gathered together at St. James's Park Newcastle for one reason and for one reason only. They wanted to know what was happening with Alan Shearer. The club's top scorer was the hero of the Toon. He was the local Geordie lad who was the captain of England. He was also one of England's few genuine world-class soccer players. He had left Newcastle to travel the length of the country to join Southampton where he made his mark with a hat trick against Arsenal at the tender age of sixteen. He had subsequently left Southampton for a then British record transfer fee of £3.5 million. The canny Scot, Kenny Dalglish, had spotted the makings of a true champion and gambled a huge sum to bring the still young Alan Shearer to Ewood Park, Blackburn. Shearer then saw fit to make Kenny proud by casually discarding the weight of the record transfer fee and scoring thirty goals in back to back seasons, a feat never before achieved. Alan Shearer was therefore not merely a Geordie gem but was also a *national* treasure. How fitting it was when Kevin Keegan, a fellow Geordie, saw fit to pay Blackburn a record £15 million to bring Shearer back to Newcastle where he had been on trial as a boy.[1]

With Shearer's help Newcastle reached second place in the championship. However this was not enough for the press, given the amount of money that Keegan had spent building the team. The pressure on Keegan to land the championship proved too much and Keegan had resigned mid-way through the season in order not to affect the upcoming stock market flotation. Ruud Gullitt, the laid-back Dutch master, had proved too laid back for Ken Bates, the Chelsea chairman, and had been sacked by the London club despite winning several trophies. Now Gullitt was in charge at Newcastle but the Geordie fans were not happy. Gullitt had fallen out with Alan Shearer and had left him out of the team. Shearer was not happy and everyone knew it. The team's results were suffering and Newcastle had slipped into the relegation zone. The situation was untenable. Either Shearer had to be sold or the manager had to go. So what happened? Well, Ruud Gullit was subsequently sacked and replaced with Bobby Robson, the ex-England manager who had gone on to success in Holland, Spain and Portugal. However, Bobby Robson was first and foremost a Geordie boy at heart. With basically the same players he not only avoided relegation, but also climbed into mid-table security and would ultimately lead them into the heights of the Champions League.[2]

In sport, results speak for themselves. If the team has not accumulated enough points during the season no amount of sophistry is going to talk a manager out of relegation. No amount of flattering the Chairman will save the manager from the fury of the fans if the team fails to win. The fans want their team to win and if the manager has to go, then so be it. The manager picks the team, therefore if the team does not perform the blame lies firmly at the door of the manager. Now that is refreshing. There are many, many business organisations that are being suffocated by inept managers. There are many managers who

---

1.   Shearer had trials with Newcastle as a boy but his potential was not spotted. This probably due to the fact that he was told to play in goal.

2.   Bobby Robson's achievements were such that he was awarded a Knighthood in 2002 and is now known as *Sir* Bobby Robson.

would actually improve the performance of their teams merely by staying away from the office.[3]

We have now spent a long time exploring the causes of the demise of the Anglo-American capitalist system. It may be unfair to lay the blame at the door of inept middle managers but there is something about the structure of the modern business enterprise that needs revisiting if the total collapse of the Anglo-American capitalist system is to be avoided. The anti-capitalist protests that erupted in 2000 and 2001 can be likened to the Newcastle fans protesting about the performance of their team. It is too simplistic to claim that the protesters were all anarchists seeking to destroy the economic system. Maybe many of them were just avid fans protesting about the unsuccessful management of their beloved team. If this is true then it is quite clear that they have a very good case.

A collapsing economy should not be looked on as a cataclysmic event. It sounds disastrous but it is not as bad as it sounds and happens more often than one might think. One only has to look at the Japanese economy since the start of the 1990s to find uncanny parallels with the United States economy, and it is only by embracing 'rock and roll economics' that the Anglo-American economies will avoid the fate inflicted on the Japanese economy. The fact that the Japanese are in total denial of their situation and continue to cling to outmoded economic medicine indicates that they would rather suffer a long and painful demise than take the actions that would restore the economy to its former glory. This shows that once an economy has grown so far so fast that it becomes full to the gills with unproductive layabouts it

---

3. An increasing number of companies now implement a 360-degree appraisal system. This entails am employee being reviewed by their peers and subordinates as well as their superiors. The purpose is to obtain a more rounded view of the employee's performance. This appraisal system allows the 'rock and roll organisation' to have a formal mechanism for airing grievances against a manager that could ultimately lead to his or her dismissal.

becomes very hard to make the changes necessary to keep the economy growing. The professionals in business and economics are under the impression that the strategies that brought success will continue to support their way of life. Unfortunately there is only so much dead weight that an economy can handle.

As far back as Plato's *Republic* it has been accepted that some others in society support certain members of society. However the laws of physics also apply to sociological structures, and when the structure becomes top-heavy it is certain to collapse. It therefore follows that if a collapse is to be avoided, an urgent re-engineering project needs to be undertaken. The aim must be to re-design the structure preserving the best parts where possible and allowing the new structure to withstand the hostilities of the external environment.

The following is an extract from www.solomon-investments.com published in December 2000:

The BOJ are singing while the Japanese economy sinks

The weakening economy, the falling Yen, the tumbling stock market, and the crumbling banking sector. With all these problems one might have thought that the Japanese authorities would be earnestly seeking to address these issues in order to generate a meaningful economic recovery.

Unfortunately this is Japan we are talking about, and eleven years after the plunge in the economy, the government and the Bank of Japan still lack the will to tackle their economic woes. They are putting short-term social stability before long-term economic health. Unfortunately the long-term has finally caught up with them and the economy is now dying.

As the Japanese economy sinks slowly below the waves, the ballast of 'free' money in the form of the near-zero interest rate policy is failing to keep it afloat. The authorities are showing an incredible indifference to the situation, and are quite happy to watch the economy sink further and further towards the bottom whilst they can be heard to blithely sing;

"*We all live in a yellow submarine, yellow submarine, yellow submarine…*"

What we must all realise is that the growth in the Japanese economy since the end of WWII was a form of 'over-achievement' on a massive scale. Japan is twenty-five times smaller than the USA in terms of geographical area, and has a population half the size.

In terms of natural resources, Japan had no right to grow to become the second largest economy in the world, and it is obviously struggling to remain there. The rest of the world is urging them to make difficult choices in order to maintain their position, but they don't want to…and why should they? With such population density they cannot afford to risk the kind of social instability that is accepted as normal in the United States. The rich people have nowhere to hide.

There is no law that states that an economy needs to grow continuously. It is not a given that the stagnant economy means that the Japanese government are failing miserably in their duty, but Adam Smith states that growth in a country (read: company) is good and leads to happiness whereas decline is bad and leads to misery. Therefore if a company were democratic, the workforce would be able to vote out the management for poor performance in the same way that shareholders can. Like Ruud Gullitt, football managers can be driven out if the relationship with the players disintegrates because of poor tactics, or a personality clash. Some people may say that there is no comparison between managing a football club and managing a modern economy. However Mrs. Thatcher often likened economic management to the way in which her father managed the grocery shop above which she was born.

To fully comprehend the purpose and structure of a business organization one must go back to how and why it came into being in the first place. Modern business and the capitalist system within which it thrives did not come about by grand design by ivory tower specialists, or from divine intervention from a supernatural being. The modern business organization was, and still is, a human attempt to solve a human problem that is at the heart of economics. That is, the question of how to manage finite resources to the best advantage. Alternatively, it is the perennial question of how to get more for less whilst respecting human dignity.

Are offices nothing more than modern-day workhouses?

In the United Kingdom, the workhouses of the 17th century were developed to offer somewhere to go for those without money or shelter. Inside the workhouse the poor exchanged their work for shelter. Initially it was voluntary but entry to the workhouse eventually became institutionalized. In the Poor Law Amendment Act of 1834 it was made a legal requirement for an individual to go to the workhouse if the person had no means of support. Workhouses were eventually abolished due to the inhumane treatment of the inhabitants, but there is a case to answer that it has been replaced by the concept of the factory and the office. Work has become voluntary again but the modern capitalist economy begs the question, does one really have a choice?

It is a given that the citizens in an economy need to do productive work in order for the economy to thrive. Adam Smith states that all wealth is a result of productive work. However it is the organization of this work that is the issue here and more importantly that the organization of the work should not be counter-productive to the economic welfare of the citizens and the country as a whole. Adam Smith also stated that the dexterity resulting from the division of work causes great improvements for the whole of society. Unfortunately for Adam Smith, humans are humans and the division of work is inhumane when taken to the extreme. Frederick Taylor claimed that 'scientific management' could achieve the optimization of even the simplest task.[4] This involved the managers specifying the detail of the task, the tools to be used and the expected performance. Higher wages would be given for superior performance and a financial disincentive for a sub-par performance. The philosophy behind this was a belief that managers and workers could work together to achieve superior long-term profits for the firm with a resultant increase in wages and job-stability for the worker. He argued that there was no need for the adversarial positioning that prevailed at the time. Unfortunately during Taylor's lifetime he did not manage to break down the confrontational mind-set that had been built up over the previous generations. Taylor's tools were made to improve worker output but the managers at the time imposed a limit on wages. This meant that the workers would not share equally in all productivity improvements. This was against Taylor's doctrine and had the effect of dehumanizing the worker to the role of an efficient machine. The resultant worker dissatisfaction caused 'scientific management' to fall out of use among practitioners.[5]

So far we can summarize that the majority of people in society have an economic need to go to work. They need to swap their work for money in order to survive, but it is important that they be treated fairly for the economic system to be sustainable. It is therefore very important that the *structure* of the organization facilitates these economic goals. There have been many attempts to define the structure of business organizations. Management theory from Frederick Taylor to Michael Porter,

---

4.   Frederick Taylor was the founding father of 'Scientific Management'. His theories were popular for some time and were gathered together in his groundbreaking book published in 1947. The theories fell into disrepute when they were taken to the extreme.

5.   The division of labour made a comeback when it was introduced at the department and company level by the popularity of Porters Value Chain analysis in the late 1980s. The primary motive was to cut costs by 'out-sourcing' non-core activities and using the lower transaction costs associated with using external firms dedicated to a particular function e.g. fleet management and recruitment agencies.

via Chandler and Tom Peters, has often tried to convey the complexity of business in terms of simple metaphors. These metaphors range from the centralized firm, the de-centralized firm, the matrix organization, the traditional pyramid structure, and the flat structure with minimum layers of management bureaucracy. These have all failed to some extent or the other because they are by definition gross simplifications of what is a very complex set of human and organizational interactions.

These concepts, 'isms', and theories are all the work of individuals seeking to understand and explain the world as they see it. They key phrase is *"as they see it."* They are all gross simplifications and contain within them biases of many different kinds at many different levels. Chaos theory attempts to understand by accepting complexity and the inherent unpredictability of the world in which we live in. Many of the 'isms' seek to predict outcomes based on models of reality that are simplifications of reality. The extent that the outcomes predicted by these models are accurate is directly related to the extent to which the 'variables' are controlled in order to *ensure* the desired outcome. Many of the 'isms' are not models at all. They are subtle ways of manipulating society at the behest of the developers and users of these models. Unfortunately this is a simplification of the real world and the extent to which a university graduate is successful in the 'real world' is dependent on his or her ability to force the world to act according to these simplified views. If it works well the graduate is further convinced of the correctness of his or her views and sees no need to change. In the graduate's opinion the people who disagree are obviously not as clever as they are. It is therefore the graduates who cause many problems because they just do what they are told without thinking. The graduates seek advancements by flattering the people in charge by showing absolute willingness to agree to their rules. In this way the psychosis of the leaders of an organization is passed down to people at the lower levels. Once this psychosis is ingrained it is very hard to dislodge without a huge paradigm shift similar to the one taking place in the financial markets at the present time.

The human fallibility, of which psychosis is only one example, means that any economic or business structure needs to have systems in place to counteract the negative effect of human fallibility. Information Technology applications increase productivity with the only limit on their successful use being the inability of computers to be truly creative. Computers are excellent at following detailed instructions but all decision-making processes must be pre-programmed. On the other hand, the Internet increases human creativity, and increases, via 'Web Services' the division of work for Information Technology applications. Therefore 'Web Services' will provide a massive leap forward in company productivity. This will create within business software the same 'winner takes all' situation that is prevailing in so many aspects of society at this time.

While we are on the subject of psychosis, Bill Gates assumes that businesses are competing like they do in the Information Technology industry.[6] However this is not the case because the Information Technology industry is an immature industry. Businesses are better off if they seek to collaborate and form cartels in order to maximize profits at the expense of the customer. The forming of cartels is of course illegal but if OPEC can get away with it there is no reason why other companies in other industries cannot form similar alliances. Only people suffering from anti-social personality disorder would want all-out war with other companies in the same business. Unfortunately the business challenge of the Information Technology era is based on the fact these immature sociopaths are beginning to dictate the pace of business. Either they will be reined in or Information Technology will win at the expense of business as a whole and the capitalist system as we know it.

Information Technology is still relatively new in business terms— therefore it was highly competitive from day one. From the beginning of the personal computer revolution, word processing applications

---

6.   *"Business @ The Speed of Thought"*

were competing with the manual and electric typewriter. The personal computers were competing with the mainframe computers. In the early days the mainframe computers were competing with the paper-based office. The competition is intense but there is profit for all the application software providers if the computer applications win out. However the application software victory will come at the expense of white-collar workers. Now that the trades unions have been muted there is little to stop and all-out victory for Information Technology. However the twist in the tale is that once Information Technology takes over business, the applications software providers will encourage the businesses to destroy each other. It is rather similar to those devious arms dealers who sell their products to both armies in a war whilst quietly developing even better weapons.

This constant, all-out war provides the background to the business and political environment that workers and consumers are contending with. However it is getting increasingly difficult for citizens to cope with the demands of the modern economy. Workers today have a constant sense of never having enough because the citizens with more seem to be constantly oppressing those with less. The overriding sense is that if one had more, life would be better. Unfortunately the pursuit of more is a futile struggle because everything is relative. There will always be someone with more. Mark McCormack stated that the mark of a great champion is dissatisfaction with one's own achievements.[7] This seems true in the business arena as well as the sporting arena and may well be a basic human characteristic. Unfortunately in the business arena this trait may well propel an individual towards the top of the organization but in a modern company subordinates always accomplish the work. Therefore the restraining factor will always be the ability of the subordinates to carry out the ever demanding will of the senior executives. Therefore the desire to achieve must be matched by the individual's ability to achieve those ends via his or her staff. It was

---

7.   *"What They Don't Teach You At Harvard Business School"*

easy in the days of slavery and forced work and a great many dynasties were built using those two age-old management methods. Today things are very much different in the modern capitalist economies and senior executives are discovering that the employees generally do not tend to share their ready acceptance of perpetual dissatisfaction.

In order to begin to design a business structure that best provides the mechanisms for producing the goods that people want at a price they are willing to pay, one must accept the fact that the business organization is a sociological entity. This chapter will describe a new type of organization that is equipped to survive and prosper in the realities of social, technological, economic, and political life as we progress through the millennium.

The structure of today's organizations is based on the 'military' metaphor but this is only one of many possible metaphors. Unfortunately it has become accepted as standard. However, the new 'country' metaphor put forward in this chapter is a very powerful alternative. Most other metaphors concentrate around the structure of the organization. The 'country' metaphor encompasses strategy, product, structure, training, culture, profits, alliances, and even how people live and work together.[8] The 'country' metaphor uses a sense of 'national pride' to encourage employees to undertake tasks that they might not otherwise do. Sporting events such as inter-company Olympics, World Cups etc are very important in this regard. This assumes that people choose their 'countries' very carefully when graduating.[9]

---

8. The 'country' metaphor is not the same as the 'political' metaphor because the 'political' metaphor assumes that the employees are out for themselves and are not really concerned with the firm.

9. This is the case in Japan because once a graduate joins a company they will be trained and that training is what gives them their unshakeable identity. The Japanese still try to maintain their 'job for life' contract therefore all graduates aspire to join the major firms such as Sony.

Now we are clear on the organizational metaphor that we are using we can clearly state that the 'rock and roll organization' fully embraces 'rock and roll economics' and is based on a new organizational structure that uses a 'country' metaphor as a shorthand description. Furthermore the 'rock and roll organization' combines the best of the Japanese lifelong employment model with the best of the Anglo-American capitalist model. In the 'rock and roll' model the firm is organized as a 'country.' The 'country' not only seeks progress and continued prosperity but is attempting to do so for the benefit of *all* the citizens. There are obviously discrete 'classes' of citizens that have differing levels of privilege but the concept of society for the benefit of society or "*government of the people, by the people, for the people*" is paramount.[10] The 'rock and roll' model is based on the flexibility of the United States economic system because it is currently seen as the most successful nation. The Roman Empire had its time. The British Empire had its time. The Japanese Empire had its time, and Nazi Germany had its time. Currently the United States is having its time but history tells us that their time will end eventually and a new economic and social model will emerge. Is it happening now, right in front of your very eyes?

When a nation state embraces the 'rock and roll organization' it will form a fractal-type structure. In this way the nation state is based on free enterprise wherein the enterprises are organized like nation states. This is similar to the fractals that are produced by 'chaos theory' computer programs.[11] Yet another way of thinking about the 'rock and roll organization' within a free enterprise society is that of 'internal federalism' whereby the business organizations are linked together by common values and organize themselves according to their own laws but within a framework of federal laws.

---

10. This is a quote from Lincoln's famous Gettysburg address.
11. The same structure is repeated within itself and as the level of magnification increases more and more fractals appear.

In the 'rock and roll organization' the training department is organized along the Oxbridge University model. It is the essence of knowledge management. 'Training' takes the best graduates and teaches them everything that is known within the firm because they have been selected as the next generation of leaders. Of course, not all the knowledge will be transferred initially because the 'rock and roll organization' must keep the value within the company. Therefore the graduate will need to pass initiation, probation, and development stages that will introduce to the graduate the unique norms and values of the 'rock and roll organization'. In this way the graduate will eventually acquire the unique core competencies that drive the functions that provide the value-added goods and services that keep the 'rock and roll organization' profitable.[12] This all assumes lifetime employment. It is a job for life but not necessarily the same job. In the 'rock and roll organization' employees need to accept that they will need to retrain during their careers. The employees will usually be graduates and they would be placed on a graduate training scheme. People are free to leave, or 'emigrate' but once a nationality has been established it will always remain, and cannot easily be changed. An employee can always change his or her 'citizenship' but the 'rock and roll organization' model accepts the power of culture and institutionalization. One cannot change even if one wants to. Another country can accept 'immigrants' if it wishes but it would have to deal with the problems of 'racism' and general inequality. Graduates may emigrate but they will become an immigrant in the host country and may not be better off. For example, a Russian scientist immigrating to America still remains a Russian scientist. The 'immigrants' would have the problem of whether to integrate or to seek to protect their own identities. This will be a very difficult decision

---

12. A firm based on the 'rock and roll' model will need to make more than one product. In 'rock and roll economics' it is folly to rely on the continued popularity of a single product. Firms will rely more on their 'core competencies.' They would become like General Electric or Microsoft. Many, many product lines, making a massive amount of money, and all the employees are stockholders.

because protecting their own identities might risk 'alienation' and force them into organizational 'ghettoes'.

Success in the 'rock and roll organization' will be measured by growth in monetary terms, and the continued contentment of the people. This is facilitated by the ability of the employees to vote for the Board of Directors, otherwise known as the 'government'. This is a complete reversal of the present Anglo-American system wherein the Board elects the Board. Presently there is no quality control and there is little that the shareholders, employees and other stakeholders can directly do to replace an under-performing Board. The shareholders must apply influence, but that takes time. Even in these cases there is seldom a complete removal of the Board except in the event of a takeover. In the 'rock and roll organization' a hostile takeover is akin to war.[13] 'War' in the form of hostile takeovers would need to become accepted. The Japanese and German economic models have still not entirely accepted the need for hostile takeovers. If a 'country' is not prospering there is likely to be a 'revolution' and its disintegration would encourage a 'war' by a rival 'country.' In some cases a 'civil war' of some description may erupt triggering a decline, which in turn precipitates an invasion by a hostile force.

Of course in the 'rock and roll organization' the CEO is tantamount to the 'king' but that goes without saying. There may even be a 'Royal Family' in a family-run business but the 'training' department would seek to ensure a meritocracy. However there is always nepotism in any society and the existence of a 'Royal Family' need not be a bad thing. The British Royal Family did not become the Royal Family by winning a popularity contest. They staked a claim, and eliminated anyone who disagreed. They then kept on eliminating dissenters until there were no dissenters left. When everyone had acquiesced, then the story

---

13. There is no direct comparison to a friendly merger at the country level. This is neither here nor there because it seems that a friendly merger is a hostile takeover by a more polite name.

went around that *"it's just the way it is."* Finally, the citizens were able to forgive the generations of elimination and claim, *"well actually, they're not that bad after all."*

A 'Royal Family' where position is based on birth rather than merit would be the exception rather than the rule, but in the 'rock and roll organization' there must be a hierarchy of some form. The trend towards de-layering and flat structures is a not-so-subtle way of cutting costs, but it needs to be accepted that hierarchies are a fact of life. For someone to be on top, someone must be on the bottom. For someone to have more, someone has to have less. With a nod to Einstein we can see that everything is relative. Therefore the whole concept of 'equality' and 'classlessness' is fatally flawed. A hierarchy exists because there are always people who not only want more, but also have a deep psychological need to have more.[14] It is this need that drives people to become successful. The notion of success is just another version of having more. For one to be successful someone else must fail. However no one *wants* to be seen as a failure so the concept of 'relative depravation' is the key to the smooth functioning of society. However 'relative depravation' is merely a way of saying, *"He has way more than I do, so he doesn't count."* Only our peer group matters for purposes of comparison. Unfortunately this allows certain groups to amass huge resources and privileges that go unseen by other groups. When this becomes apparent we have an increase in what Marx would call class conflict. For instance, the dot-com fraud was just another example of class conflict because the fraudsters thought that it was acceptable to steal from investors but needless to say the investors did not agree. The 'rock and

---

14. Maslow identified five layers of psychological needs in the form of a pyramid. One may argue about there being exactly five discrete layers of needs that an individual progresses through on the ay of 'self-actualisation' but in terms of explaining how some people are willing and able to accept levels of need that are fulfilling for them but would not fulfil the needs and desires of other people. It is this concept that drives some people to achievements that other people do not desire or even deem necessary.

roll organization' will need executives appointed as much for their *ethics* as their business expertise. They will be needed to supply the integrity that is so obviously currently lacking in the business world at the present time.

The 'rock and roll organization' will not be susceptible to the kind of executive fraud that so gripped many companies in the late 1990s. This is because the 'rock and roll organization' is based on binary logic and not sophistry. In modern western society it is the sophisticated people who are in charge. In government, the law, business and education, the sophisticates dictate what is good or bad, right and wrong. Everybody else is told to go along with it because the sophisticated people know best. The problem for society is that the word 'sophisticated' originates from the Greek word 'sophis.' Sophistry is defined as a "*fallacious reasoning.*" 'Fallacious' is defined as "*an incorrect, misleading opinion or argument.*" Therefore to be sophisticated is to have the ability to argue a logically flawed opinion, usually designed to convince and deceive the masses.[15] In this amorphous mass of multi-cultural identity there is nothing that seems to bind the citizens together. There is nothing that is, except sophistry. Sophistry is the new religion. Sophistry is the new god. Sophistry is the ability to spout a stream of utter nonsense, in the vain belief that it is meaningful and worth the time invested by the listener. People who have lost their identity in the pursuit of material goals have come together under the banner of sophistry. There you will find the ex-Socialists, the ex-Tories, the ex-Catholics, the ex-Muslims, the ex-Jews, and the ex-Christians. The people who have abandoned their belief systems and walked away from the life they once knew are now lost in a sea of sophistry. They are drowning in a deluge of diatribe, and as the people cry out for relief, they find none. They find

---

15. A classic example was the invasion of Iraq by the United States-led 'coalition' in order to eliminate the threat of weapons of mass-destruction. However, everyone knew Iraq did not possess weapons of mass-destruction. The reasoning failed to convince the United Nations but it was enough to convince the British parliament.

none because no one speaks the same language. No one understands the same culture. The sophists' unique social and cultural background has left them rudderless is a sea of self-obsession.

Rock and Roll Marketing

Big business is quite often concerned with making an unbelievably bad proposition easily accessible and using marketing to entice people to sign on the dotted line. The goal is to make them happy to be exploited. This is achieved by the massaging of perception and reality. Some people think that perception is reality but that is not true. Reality is what is. Perception is what one perceives. In an ideal world the two would be the same. However in the modern world of mass advertising and marketing gibberish, the reality has become lost and all we have is perception. It is a very dangerous situation when we are told that the marketing gibberish is reality. If it were reality there would be no need for marketing. Consumers would surely buy the product unprompted because the product is really as good as others claim it to be.

Maybe the sophistry got out of control when a former actor was elected President of the United States. An actor needs the audience to suspend belief. A good actor is able to convince the audience that the character being portrayed is real. This way the movie or play works. If the actor is not able to do this, the movie does not work and the actor is said to be a bad actor. Therefore the world obviously arrived at a situation whereby Ronald Reagan was 'pretending' to be President of the United States and obviously convincing the American public. This coincided with the whole 1980s marketing revolution where style mattered more than content. We are still living with that legacy today, but the world desperately needs a reality-check.

The importance of the Information Technology revolution has been obscured by the fact that at the same time that the microchip revolution was taking place, there was an upsurge in sophistry. With Ronald Reagan in the White House, the 1980s marked a huge increase in the power of advertising. Marketing became the new religion. The ability to endow a company's products with imaginary powers of sex appeal, culture, and other life-style enhancing attributes became more important than the product itself. Style over content went from being a slur on products and the organizations that produced them, to becoming the slogan that legitimized the whole process. Everybody *knew* that style was more important than content, so surely it was rational to concentrate more on style than content. It just made good business sense. Now style is out of fashion, and content is king. There is only one reality. Everything else is a fantasy. People are generally miserable because they are forced to live their lives as a fantasy, and they dislike it intensely. They really do want reality. They can handle it. People know where they are in a world of reality. One knows whom one can trust and whom one cannot trust. One does not need to smile as one is being exploited.

The Geeks Inherit The Earth

The need for reality goes hand-in-hand with the predominance of the personal computer. The two things are linked because the microchip revolution is based on the same logic that Socrates, the nemesis of the sophists, used in ancient Greece. It is based on zeroes and ones, true and false, right and wrong. It is based on the fact that there *is* a right answer if only we work through the logic carefully enough. The sophisticates do not like this world of contrasts, the world of black and white of you like. It is no coincidence that business and government people previously lived in a grey world. A world of grey suits, grey hair, and grey buildings. They did not believe in black and white, they did not believe in right and wrong, and they certainly did not believe in good and evil. The personal computer revolution destroyed that world and now the Internet revolution is burying it forever. Computers are great at calculating and processing very fast and accurately. However they cannot create, they cannot think. That is where humans have the edge. Unfortunately for the middle-class their whole structure was built on them having inside knowledge of the workings of the organization. The information was reported back to the upper classes. They held the knowledge and therefore the power. There was a 'moral-hazard' in place but Information Technology revolutionizes this situation. For instance, a computer can transfer money from one bank account to another without the worry of it being stolen. This is true for £10m as easily as it is true for £10. The middle-class was employed because they could be trusted *more* than the working-class. The middle-class still had to be checked but they could be trusted *up to a point.* The problem being that even all humans have their limit and eventually the temptation to steal would prove too much. They would not steal £10, maybe not £100 or £1000 or £10,000, but when you get to £100,000 or £1,000,000 society finds that it has a problem. The employee only needs to get away with it once. The same holds true for bribery that seldom talked about cost of doing business. Everybody has their hand out and the 'perks' are treated as part of the salary. However, computers do not take or pay bribes. They do what they are told, only what they are told, and only when they are told. Furthermore, computers do not ask for pay-rises. In this way they are the ideal employees. Once the software has been developed, the cost per usage falls exponentially. However there is a limit to the use and spread of Information Technology applications. The move to more Information Technology and less paper-based checking assumes a fraud-free business environment. Unfortunately fraud is a part of business life and many forms exist to prevent it. Business processes are slower as a result but otherwise businesses are *asking* to be cheated.

Many Information Technology initiatives provide a one-off boost to earnings in year one over year zero. However by year two the need to beat year one earnings means that the value of the benefits is now zero because the money is already in the bank. This demonstrates that it is only the *structure* of systems and performance incentives that really drive profits and organizational performance. The majority of Information Technology initiatives at the present time are merely examples of corporate penny-pinching.

In this corporate and economic restructuring some of the middle classes will be upgraded to join the upper class while the rest will be downgraded to re-join the working classes whence they came. No one said that life was fair. It is because of the almost genetic desire to get something for nothing that has made the position of the middle-class professionals in modern organizations untenable. It is the conflict between Major Ingram and 'Gordon Gekko.'[16] Major Ingram and his wife wanted something for nothing. Mrs. Ingram and her brother had previously been a contestant on Millionaire and had both won £32,000. This obviously was not enough for Mrs. Ingram as she was the instigator behind the 'Major Fraud.' She roped her husband into the scam because they both knew that he was not intelligent enough to win a big money prize by fair means. 'Gekkoism' had possessed the Ingrams. They were consumed by pure greed. Financially, they were in dire straits and they had identified Millionaire as a source of money for nothing. However they had not reckoned on the designers of the quiz show. The designers had designed a game where it was almost impossible to win the big prize. They had designed a game whereby if the contestant were intelligent enough to answer the more difficult questions, they would be unlikely to answer the apparently trivial questions. The designers know that it is unlikely that a person who reads about Faust would also watch 'Friends.' It is unlikely that a person who watches 'Baywatch' will also be listening to Beethoven. Furthermore an error

---

16. Major Ingram, his wife, and Teclan Whittock were convicted in April 2003 in the UK for trying to defraud Celedor the makers of "Who Wants To Be A Millionaire" out of £1m. The criminals established a system of coughs to indicate the correct answer to the idiot Major in the hot seat. That he was cheating was obvious if only because it was quite clear that he had barely enough intelligence to tie his own shoelaces.

on the £500,000 question means that the contestant drops down 'snakes and ladders' style to the £32,000 level. This means that at the latter stages it is total madness to proceed with the questions unless the contestant absolutely *knows* the answer. Any Millionaire winner would therefore need to be very clever, very determined, and very, very lucky.

When it comes to communication in the 'rock and roll organization' nothing quite as basic as coughs and splutters are needed. 'Gangsta rap' is the new method of communication for business and politics because the old military warfare metaphor has evolved into a new form that can best be described as 'gang warfare.' The 'military' metaphor assumed two sides of either individual countries or allies of countries. The 'gang warfare' metaphor assumes numerous 'gangs' competing over turf. Alliances are temporary and treachery is the norm. The turf is the customer base. Products and services are the weapons and increased money and power is the goal. Survival is only for as long as one can stay alive. Death is accepted as part of the game and the dream is to get out of the ghetto, but no one escapes except in a body bag.

The goal of the 'gang warfare' metaphor is to teach the middle-class how to survive the new realities of life after they have been betrayed by the upper class. The ruling classes never liked them and have replaced them with Information Technology. The middle-class and the working-class now have to slug it out. Unfortunately the middle-classes have never been taught how to fight. They have expected life on a plate at the expense of the working class but now the working class has been released from their sociological prison and they are as mad as hell. The 'prison guards' will be the first to go as the rioting escalates. It may seem like anarchy but it is merely 'gang warfare.' The sociology and psychology of gangs becomes paramount to understanding society. When the President has sex with an intern in the White House and does not lose his job because the people think it is normal, we have all got to come to terms with the new reality. Reality is the buzzword. No more spin, no more gibberish. A lie is a lie, and fraud is fraud. The lawyers are waiting and litigation takes the place of an AK47. "*Let's keep it real*" is the slogan sweeping the accountancy profession. We all know the tricks now, and no one is fooled. The Internet *did* change everything after all.

Capitalism is primarily concerned with providing the goods and services that people want at a price that they are willing to pay. It does not say anything about creating jobs for people. Having a job is not a given. It is not a right. The onus is on the employee to be beneficial to the organization over and above the cost of employment. It was not inevitable that the middle-class will systematically written out of the script that is Anglo-American capitalism. There is no reason why they will not able to adapt Darwin-like to the changing environment and maintain their position in the class structure. However it seems that the years of having it easy has left the middle-class with a soft underbelly that is preventing them from withstanding the 'rocking and rolling' of the new realities. The years of getting something for nothing and not just getting something for nothing, but feeling that they had a *right* to get something for nothing, have turned the middle-class into the lumbering dinosaurs of the capitalist system. The years of presiding, like Victorian prison guards, over the exploitation of the working-class are well and truly over. The days are well and truly over when the only qualification for a management position was the ability to turn away and close one's ears to the cries of anguish from the oppressed masses.

Capitalism versus Cannabis

Many people are 'accidental capitalists' insofar as they have bought into the capitalist system by default. They did not choose it but there appears to be no alternative. They work in a system that in some cases they despise. They do not necessarily agree with the capitalist ideals but they are stuck with them.

However it seems that increasingly people from all walks of life are turning to an alternative. Harmless or not harmless—that is the question, but it does seem that a regular intake of cannabis reduces the user's ability to participate in the capitalist system. The effect of the drug makes it very difficult to get to work by 09:00 and makes it difficult to be concerned about the consequences. Now that cannabis has been 'de-criminalized' in the United Kingdom it now sits squarely at odds with the spirit of capitalism in the modern sense. In one corner humans are treated, and expected to behave, like machines. Any deviance is punished and standardization and conformity is rewarded. In the other corner 'dope' sets the mind free and opens doors through which, once passed, it is impossible to return. The question is which state is the correct state of existence for a human being? Which state sits in harmony with the human condition, and which state is its antithesis? Whatever the answer is, it is quite clear that the alternative should indeed be made illegal. Either 'de-criminalizing' cannabis is a fatal mistake that will destroy the human and economic condition and the ability of people to live in harmony with their environment, or it is a small step for man and a giant leap for mankind.

What needs to be understood is that crime is a sociological concept. Society as a whole cannot put all citizens in prison; therefore, if a large number of citizens indulge in illegal substances, then society must by definition make the substance legal. By forcing cannabis to be 'de-criminalized' society has, in effect, caused capitalism to be 'criminalized.'

9

The Age of Aquarius

"Are you having fun yet?" he bellowed. The answer was an unmitigated "no" but no one dared to reply to the question. This may have been due to the fact that the questioner was a frighteningly imposing figure. He looked like Lennox Lewis, the world heavyweight-boxing champion, and was built the same way. His dreadlocks flowed down to the centre of his back despite some being tied up in a ponytail. The white t-shirt that he was wearing had the logo "*Cool Runnings*" on the chest but no one was cool and no one was running. The t-shirt barely managed to contain the man's muscles that were now clearly visible due to the soaking that he was getting. "Are you having fun, yet?" he shouted again. Unfortunately for the group of holidaymakers the only person having fun was the Lennox-Lewis look-alike. He seemed to take a sadistic pleasure from the fact that he was scaring the hell out of the people in the group.

The scene was Dunns River Falls in Jamaica. The holidaymakers had gathered to climb the waterfall at Dunns River. Many of them had mistakenly believed that they were going to take a leisurely stroll up the side of the cliff that formed the waterfall. Some had thought that they might even have the opportunity to stand in the waterfall and take a few holiday snaps. The tour representatives had said that they would climb Dunns River Falls—and climb it they would. One by one they took tentative steps across the slippery rocks. They had been told to hold hands in a giant human chain. Apparently this was for their safety but many people wondered if the whole episode was safe at all. The holidaymakers were not only desperately trying to negotiate their own passage through the slippery rocks but they were also watching out for the person in front. If the person in front were to fall it would bring down the next person, causing the whole human chain to collapse like a set of sun-drenched, water-soaked, bloodstained dominoes.

Onward they climbed, holding on to each other for dear life, keeping each other from falling more out of self-preservation than altruism. Under the low ceiling they went. One tall holidaymaker had smashed his head against the low overhanging rock despite the repeated warnings to *"Mind your head!"* He left the group and wandered back towards the Lennox Lewis look-alike, hoping for some assistance. Unfortunately for him he got no assistance and even less sympathy. The blood flowed from a gash in his head that was only revealed when he removed his baseball hat. He looked a mess but the other holidaymakers looked upon him as a walking warning and concentrated even harder on minding their heads.

"Go to the right! Up against the wall." The requests were not requests any longer. They were orders and they were being barked out with increasing ferocity as the Jamaican voices fought to be heard over the noise of the waterfall. The holidaymakers groped against the sheer, slime covered wall in order to find the finger holes that provided the only method of avoiding being swept away. Fun this was not. It had ceased to be fun some time ago. It was now a battle for survival. It was now merely about getting back safely without a broken leg or a twisted ankle. One holidaymaker spotted an exit half way up the waterfall and attempted to make his way towards it. *"Get back over there!"* he was ordered, and he had to comply. There was no disagreeing or discussion with these tour guides. They were more like concentration camp guards than tour guides and the holidaymakers realised they had to obey.

The holidaymakers realised that they had to obey because ultimately what they were doing was dangerous, unnecessary and unnatural. The water was flowing *down* the waterfall in order to get to the ocean. What on earth the holidaymakers were doing climbing *up* the waterfall was a total mystery to the tour guides. Why people would risk injury for the apparent thrill of climbing the raging water at Dunns River Falls was beyond their comprehension, but they came every day by the coach load. The tour guides were there to make sure that the holidaymakers would complete the climb as safely as possible—but surely they would have been better off merely relaxing on the beach! Natural logic versus human logic, you pay your money and you take your choice.

On reaching the top of the waterfall the scene was one of overwhelming joy and relief. Partners hugged each other and smiles returned to the faces. Why do humans do this to themselves? After all, the waterfall did not *need* to be climbed. That it was a beautiful and powerful natural phenomenon was there for all to see. One could take a leisurely stroll up the path adjacent to the waterfall and walk all the way to the top. But no, we are talking about human beings here. Furthermore, we are talking about human beings on holiday, and human beings on holiday want to have *fun*. The fact that fun involves risking life and limb and scaring oneself half to death is something for the psychologists to ponder. Fortunately for everyone, 'rock and roll economics' accepts the fact that humans are generally irrational and in some cases outright self-destructive.

This last chapter is called "The Age of Aquarius" and Aquarius is the sign of the Zodiac that follows Capricorn and precedes Pisces. However, the term "Age of Aquarius" refers not to the charts of the Zodiac but to the fact that Aquarius is the sign of the Water Carrier. The Age of Aquarius is therefore named because the age in which we are now living reflects the importance of water. We have seen the importance of 'chaos theory' in understanding the world in which we live and that the investigations that led to the 'chaos theory' came from the study of fluid dynamics. The Age of Aquarius reflects the fact that water is extremely important to the natural and human condition.[1] The Age of Aquarius brings the properties of water to the forefront of management and economic decision-making.

It is the fluid properties of water that concerns us here. Specifically it is the way in which water flows downhill. It is the way in which rainfall collects in a highland region and begins to flow downwards. It is the way in which the force of gravity pulls the water back whence it came. The water *must* get back to the ocean. The water *will* get back to the ocean. The only issue of doubt is *how* the water will get back to the ocean. The goal is pre-determined and fixed. The direction is fixed, and irreversible. The only thing to be decided is the *course* that the water will travel on its way to the ocean.

However, the best way to illustrate the Age of Aquarius is to tell the story of the publication of this book. This book needed to be written and it needed to be published. The public want reality and it is not given to them. Book sales have generally fallen in recent years because people simply no longer have the time to read. The book-buying public do not have the time to read garbage and they certainly are not going to pay for the privilege. They will watch a movie, or listen to a CD, but who has time these days to read a book? Therefore this book was written for the MTV generation. It is short, sharp, direct and full of energy. The public love it even if the establishment do not. It therefore needed to be published in order that the audience can decide its merits. It is the audience who decide what is good or bad, not the critics. In this way, it was imperative that *Rock and Roll Economics* reached

---

1.   The surface of the earth and the average human being is predominately composed of water.

its audience one way or the other. Like a river flowing to the ocean, it will take the path of least resistance, smashing through any man-made obstacles. The fact that you are reading this now means that it was successful, but at the time of writing that success is not guaranteed and the route to that success is as yet unknown. So let us see what happened?

The Texere Scenario

Well, we are into June now and that means that the deadline has been missed. The promise was that the first draft would be completed by the end of May. Fortunately it did not appear that the publisher was too keen to receive the finished manuscript. David Wilson at Texere had liked the sample chapter and had said that it was "*superb.*" David Wilson had previously worked for Wiley & Sons in Chichester and Rachel Wilkie at Wiley had given David's name as a possible alternative after Wiley had rejected the sample chapter. Wiley did not like "*The Hypocrisy of Modern Finance*" and probably hoped that the book would never see the light of day. The women at Wiley just wanted an easy life. They had a cushy number down in leafy Chichester and had no desire to see their boat rocked or rolled in even the slightest way.

"*Very powerful,*" she had said in the rejection letter—the same phrase she had used three times when speaking on the telephone three days earlier. "*Very powerful*"—but obviously not right to sit on one of Wiley's prestigious book lists. They had published two of Soros' previous books so it could have been assumed that they would have liked the content and the style, but Wiley were not interested in any of that. All they wanted was a 'name.' A 'name' would sell books. That was it in a nutshell. A 'name' is guaranteed to move units *regardless* of the content. The book can be garbage but if the author is a 'name' then the publishers will out-bid each other for the honour of publishing the book. Of course the audience do not want to *read* garbage and the book will not sell, losing the publisher money. This is acceptable for the publishing employee because backing a 'name' means that the employee does not need to do any work. It goes without saying that the women at Wiley are all frighteningly middle-class. Their collective goal is to get something for nothing and they do not want to go to the effort of reading, understanding, and assessing a book before determining the book's marketability. This is because reading manuscripts would get in the way of the real work of the day. What it is that they do remains a mystery. It is not even possible to make a joke about it because one would need some raw material in order to create a joke about the working day of the Wiley women. Unfortunately no joke is possible because no one has a clue as to what it is they do.

Anyway, that is enough about the Wiley women. Rachel Wilkie at least had enough wherewithals to suggest when prompted that Texere may be a viable alternative. After a brief look at the website it seemed that Texere might indeed be the right publisher for this book. However there could be one snag. The book highlighted on the Texere website was *Sex, Drugs & Economics* by Diane Coyle. The book seems to be an attempt to dumb down and popularise the standard economic fare that already turns off men and women across the globe. Her book is a fair attempt to convince the unconvinced that economics is relevant to their day to day lives and that a thorough understanding of the subject will enhance and enrich the reader to such an extent that he or she will wonder how they ever managed to survive so long without the enlightenment that comes from economic theory. Diane's book is about as far as an Oxford/Harvard trained economist can go, but one thing is for sure, it is *not* rock and roll.

The key to the acceptance of *Rock and Roll Economics* by Texere is whether or not they would allow a new book by a new author that so directly opposes the thrust of one of their existing books. It would be very brave of Texere and give credibility to *Rock and Roll Economics*—but would they do it? Would their nerve hold? We would find out eventually but one thing is sure, *Rock and Roll Economics* did not need the stamp of approval from Texere or Wiley. *Rock and Roll Economics* would find its way to the people like a river finds its way to the ocean.

Bloody Agents

"Here's my card," said Chris Eubank. The former world-boxing champion smiled his strange smile. His hands were thinner than one would expect but they probably still packed a punch. I smiled back. We were on the seafront in Brighton. It was whilst driving along the seafront that Eubank's car was spotted. It had one of his not very subtle 'KO' number plates on the vehicle. Chris Eubank is not known to be the most quiet and reserved person in the world and it is usually quite obvious when he is around. I approached a couple of black guys at the top of the steps leading to the beach and asked if they had seen him. They replied that he was around somewhere. I walked down the steps and gazed along the beach. Of course, I should have known. He was standing by a bench talking to a couple of women. The women were sitting down but Eubank was standing on what appeared to be a child's scooter. He had been scooting around Brighton beach just doing what he does best, annoying many of the other residents of the town by just being Chris Eubank. Thankfully he had stopped scooting because I did not want to flag him down. I had met him previously on several occasions. The first time was when he was driving his huge American truck through the centre of town. It seemed to take up the whole road and it looked as though that some crazed trucker had taken a wrong turn. On closer inspection one could see the 'KO' number plate and it was obvious who it was. He had stopped to jump out and chat to a couple of women so I took the opportunity to talk with him.

This time, however, on Brighton seafront, there was no time to chat so it was kept brief. We thought that there would be opportunities in the future to do some business together and we swapped telephone numbers. He also gave me his business card. The contact card had the name and contact details of his agent, one Alon Shulman of World Famous Limited in London. The card was put in a safe place on the assumption that it would prove useful at some point. A couple of years later it was placed on the office desk in anticipation of the completion of *Rock and Roll Economics*. The time had come to make the telephone call.

After putting the phone down the realisation came that it may have been a mistake. It was impossible to get a word in. Alon Shulman was Jewish so one can assume that he was talking *spiel*. Whatever it was, it went on and on and on. It is safe to call it sophistry but it was not entirely convincing. Apparently the agent had himself written a book called *The Style Guide* in the late 1990s that had sold well and he also *claimed* to have negotiated a significant advance for David Beckham's book. He was asked whether he had been involved in Chris Eubank's book and he said he had but unfortunately it had not been published. Shulman said that basically any book can get published—it is just a matter of finding the right publisher, and he had links with many of the top publishers. And so it went. After he had finished his *spiel* I had a headache. It all sounded positive, but rather too positive. It is notoriously difficult to get a book published no matter what its merits. Therefore it was all taken with a pinch of salt. Time would tell whether he was a talker or a doer. Soon he would be asked to put up or shut up.

The procedure was this. Shulman wanted to see a synopsis of the book along with the author's resume, at which time he would discuss the merits of the book with his colleagues. He would then make a decision as to which publishers to approach. It was suggested that he could be sent a copy of the manuscript to read as that would give him a better idea as to the content and marketability of the book, but he declined the offer. Of course, that was too easy. It would also involve Shulman actually *reading* the book and, of course, that is too much like hard work. Well, the inevitable happened and after a lengthy consultation Shulman said that he could not do anything with the proposal and that the book should be taken back to Texere because they had expressed an interest. However, he did hint that Texere would only clarify that they are rejecting the book. His suggestion was that Texere were merely hoping that the book did not get completed so that they would not need to make a decision on it.

Take it To The BBC

It was Tuesday May 21 2003 and the queue was about forty deep so the first part of the plan had failed. The plan was to be first in the queue. The auditions were to start at 09:30 and the taxi was to be there all day for two days. Fortunately there were two taxis but that did not seem to make the queue move any faster. The people had gathered because the BBC was looking for talent. The annual search had the BBC looking among the general public for individuals to fulfil their dreams by working for the BBC. The rationale was unclear and maybe it was merely a gimmick. However, it had been running for several years and the brochure that came through the post seemed to offer proof that several people had indeed found a successful start to careers with the BBC by applying to BBC Talent. The opportunities over the previous years had ranged from behind the scenes engineers to video directors to television presenters. This year they were looking for, among others, an expert to present a programme on the new digital channel BBC4. It was to be a factual programme with the aim of bringing a particular subject to life for the general public. They were not looking for television presenting experience. They were looking for that unique character, the expert in archaeology, architecture, or even anthropology, who could "*entertain and enlighten with intelligence and charm.*" That sounded easy enough. After all, business and finance do not, for most people, constitute the most riveting subject in the world. The fact that it is so vitally important to the whole well being of society is neither here nor there. The majority of people find it as infuriatingly complex as they find it incredibly boring.

Well that was then and this is now. The opportunity was there, it was genuine and it had to be exploited. The plan was to finish the book as much as possible using the BBC Talent day as the focus point. Whatever was not finished would have to wait. The auditions were to take place in mobile 'taxi' studios with the hopefuls being given one minute to do their piece to camera. Sixty seconds is not a long time to convince any prospective television producer but if a copy of the book could be left with the BBC staff then the book could prove the deciding factor and this would take the pressure off the need for a fantastic performance in front of the camera. Investigations had revealed that the BBC was not merely looking for a new television programme, but that they were primarily looking for *ideas* for television programmes. There was every possibility that if the BBC could not find a new presenter with a good idea that they would take the idea and give it to another presenter, new or otherwise. In this light it became clear that the book was the perfect pitch. The timing was right, the content was factual, and to say that the author is a character is the understatement of the year.

As I found my way to the front of the queue I realized that the taxis were situated right opposite the Brighton Dome and that the whole exercise was being conducted during the Brighton Festival. It was at The Dome during the previous year's Brighton Festival that I had the opportunity to speak to a real-life central banker. He was Belgian and was there to promote his latest book about the future of money. The thrust of the book was the idea that alternative forms of payment and compensation would increasingly be needed in modern society. It all sounded quite reasonable and was probably quite right. However we are still some way off from cleaning each other's cars in exchange for baby-sitting each other's children, and until that time most people will not be giving up on the green folding stuff just yet.

After the main debate the sponsors had allowed certain people access to a reception area where the protagonists would be popping in at some point. The Belgian central banker had shared the stage with Will Hutton but Will Hutton had stayed a short while before leaving. He did not appear to like the idea of hanging around chatting to people when he could be desperately trying to convince Tony Blair that he should have lamb chops for dinner. Will Hutton seemed to be in a hurry to attend some earth-shatteringly important engagement, but then again he always seems pre-occupied with something or the other.

The conversation between the central banker and our small group ranged across a number of subjects including Warren Buffett and the fact that he has collected rather a lot of money for himself and as yet, despite his advanced age, has not seen fit to redistribute his wealth to selected charities, as is the usual custom. Even Bill Gates has found the time to get passionate about Africa and has donated large sums to various noble causes. So maybe the Belgian central banker was onto something. If the mega-rich continue to hoard their money, maybe the poor will need to find some other way of paying for their goods and services because there will not be enough money to go around. Eventually, the subject got around to a certain George Soros and the conversation went a little like this:

CB: "Where are you from?"

MS: "That depends how far you want to go back. I was born in the UK, but my parents were from the West Indies, but of course I am originally from Africa."

CB: "Where in the West Indies are they from?"

MS: "Jamaica."

CB: "I live in the Cayman Islands."

MS: "Oh yes. Right next door. I've always thought it would be fun to pop over and maybe I would see George Soros walking to the Laundromat."

CB: "George Soros doesn't walk to the Laundromat."

MS: "Oh, of course not. He'd probably take a helicopter."

CB: *[Laughs]*

MS: "Do you know George Soros personally?"

CB: "Yes I do."

MS: "What is he like as a person? Is he a good man?"

CB: "Well yes. He's a philanthropist. He gives a lot of money away."

MS: "But if he is going to give it away, why does he collect it in the first place?"

CB: "Well, he would say that there are inefficiencies in the economic system and if he does not exploit them, someone else would."

MS: "That's all very well and good but if you rewind to 1992 when he took the Bank of England for £1bn, you will find that the government subsequently had to put VAT on domestic fuel in order to restore the public finances, and for his sake I hope that no pensioners subsequently died of hypothermia because they could not afford to heat their homes.[2] If anyone did, Soros would have blood on his hands and no amount of philanthropy will wash the blood away. I do not have any evidence but I am sure that if you check back you will find that at least one little old lady was found dead slumped over a three-bar electric fire."

Laughter erupted in the group and we swiftly moved on to the merits or otherwise of book publishing.

---

2. VAT or Value Added Tax is the United Kingdom equivalent of the United States sales tax.

Let's Put On The Show Right Here

If all else fails we could just do it ourselves. Of course, that would be the epitome of 'rock and roll economics.' We know what the people want because we have been giving it to them via the Internet for years. By bypassing the conventional publishing routes we have managed to create a global brand of huge impact that has gone largely unknown to those outside of the small band of investors. We could always start the website up again and sell the book directly. The only problem with this scenario is the printing and acceptance of payment. We would want the book to look as if it could sit on the bookshelf of a High Street bookstore and we definitely want to get paid for it, so if we could overcome these two obstacles then we could just do it ourselves. No agents to persuade to read the book. No publishers to convince. No store buyers to bribe. If the book is good it will stand or fall on its own merits and it will sell via word of mouth. After all, that was how the website started. Word of mouth had brought the readers in. Word of mouth had increased the hit count. There was no marketing needed because the product was that good. The only problem was that over the Internet the product was free. That is why the website had to stop. The people logging on to www.solomon-investments.com were verifying that they liked what they were reading and wanted more. In some cases they had *demanded* more in quite an abusive manner. That is how the idea for the book was born. If they want more we should give them more, but they must pay for the privilege. The rules of capitalism may be being rewritten but one rule still remains, that being that the producer needs the profit incentive in order to justify producing the goods that people want at a price that they are willing to pay.

So the plan was hatched. Close down the website and produce the information in book form. People still pay for books and in this way the work would reach a wider audience, resulting in a higher profile for the website. This would create a virtuous circle that would produce more sales and so on and so forth. It sounded good in theory, but would it work? There was only one way to find out. The book must be written and one way or the other it will find its way to the people. Or, as Kevin Costner famously said, *"build it and they will come."*[3]

What's It Gonna Be, Stud?

Well, the first thing that needs to happen is that the book needs to be finished. It is still only the first draft but as yet no one has seen a finished draft. It looks as if the self-publishing route using print on demand is the most likely option but the publisher must be presented with a finished draft.[4] The publisher that has been lined up provides an editing service but it is impetrative that whichever course the book takes, the tone of the book survives intact.

Although the self-publishing route is the simplest and preferred option it is by no means the *best* option. The *best* option would be for the book to be picked by Texere or alternatively published through one of the other large mainstream publishers. However, the vested interests of the publishers concerned makes this route much more difficult. For instance, the Texere route is complicated not only by the presence of Diane Coyle but also by the fact that Myles, David Wilson's partner, worked on Soros' book while he was at Wiley. He is apparently acquainted with Soros and it is quite certain that he would not want to jeopardize his relationship with the billionaire by being seen to support a book that suggests that he may be a hypocrite. It is equally certain that Soros himself would not mind such a relatively mild accusation as he has probably been on the receiving end of far more derogatory accusations.

---

3. This quote is from the movie *"Field of Dreams"* released in 1992?
4. This technique obviates the need for a large initial print run by literally enabling the publisher to print copies of the book as required.

If David, Myles and Diane Coyle have not been as helpful as they could have been, then at least there was David Boyle. Now David Boyle was also at the London Book Fair. I had popped along on the second day especially to meet Diane Coyle. Unfortunately, Myles was monopolising Diane's time. He appeared to be boring her senseless with his usual nonsense. However this was not my opinion but the opinion of his wife who also worked at Texere. She and Myles had met at Wiley and she was used to his tedious ramblings. She looked disconcerted has he waffled away to Diane and she and I spoke instead. We were at the same table as Myles and Diane but our conversations hardly mixed. Eventually Myles's wife got fed up of being ignored by Myles and it was obvious to her that I really wanted to speak to Diane. Anyway, David Wilson was hovering nearby when David Boyle entered. A bespectacled, academic looking type, he seemed quite jovial as he took the empty seat. Diane and he chatted briefly before I introduced myself. I produced the manuscript (then entitled *A New Organisation For A New Millennium*). He skimmed the pages for a few seconds before asking, "Why don't you call it 'Rock and Roll Economics'?" I feigned ignorance before turning to David Wilson and repeating the question. Wilson murmured something about titles constantly changing but offered little else. What neither Wilson or Boyle knew was that the title was always meant to be "*Rock and Roll Economics*" but the suggestion needed to come from Texere because of the potential confusion with the title of Diane Coyle's book. David Boyle did not seem to share Texere's reservation.[5]

Boyle took an immediate interest in the manuscript even though at this time I did not have any idea who he was. He did say that he had written a book and that it was in a similar tone to "*The Hypocrisy of Modern Finance*" chapter and that he was interested in reading the finished

---

5. His own book entitled "*The Sum of Our Discontent*" was not on the Texere stand because Harper Collins publishes it in the United Kingdom whereas Texere publishes the book in the United States.

chapters that I had with me. I took his contact details and allowed him to take one of the two copies that I had hoped to give away that day. This was a coup but I wondered whether anything would come of it. That David Boyle was present at the London Book Fair that day was pure good fortune because Diane Coyle, the original target, has not proved very helpful at all.[6]

It was left for a week or two before trying to contact him. Unfortunately it seemed that he was never at home. His charming sounding wife seemed very apologetic as day after day she was forced to admit that she did not know where her husband was and whether or not he was coming home. David Boyle had stood for election to Parliament in the May 2001 elections and it seemed that he had not totally forgone his political ambitions. He was still working MP's hours in an attempt to gain the support necessary for another bid. It would certainly be a big plus if he found the book interesting.

He had left a voicemail on the office telephone after the first call and over at least a week the messages were going backwards and forwards without the two parties being able to speak. It is the curse of modern technology. Eventually we did speak and it was suggested that I travel up to London to meet with him so that we could discuss the book.

It was originally hoped that David Boyle could help get *Rock and Roll Economics* published through Harper Collins, but therein lies a problem because Harper Collins have just published the new book from Baroness Margaret Thatcher called *Statecraft* in which she is unashamedly unapologetic about her policies when in power. It is not sure how Harper Collins will feel about a book that claims that Margaret Thatcher may have been, shall we say, "misguided" in some aspects of

---

6. Diane still has not responded to the chapters that were mailed to her after a meeting at the London Book Fair in March 2003. It must be assumed that she did not like the content or the inference that he lifelong devotion to economic theory was frankly pointless.

her political philosophy. In *Statecraft* she continues to wax lyrical about Adam Smith but that is not necessarily a bad thing as the famous economist has been mentioned several times in this book. However there is a point in the *Wealth of Nations* that Adam Smith states that motherhood is the *"lowest rank"* and it is clear that with more and more women postponing marriage and motherhood in pursuit of careers it is clear that for many women motherhood does not come very high in the pecking order of career choices. The fact that Diane Coyle took the opportunity at the London Book Fair to show pictures of her two wonderful children, Adam and Rufus, shows that she does not agree with Adam Smith on this point.[7]

It Never Rains But It Pours

Before we go any further we need to recap on the key factor in the success of the Age of Aquarius approach. That the river gets to the ocean eventually by some path or another is a fact. That the river gets to the ocean at all is *not* a fact. There are many, many, dried up riverbeds in highlands and lowlands alike. There are many beautiful babbling brooks that just disappear into nothingness. The countryside is littered with them. The key factor in the Age of Aquarius is persistent precipitation. It is the fact that it just keeps on raining. In fact, it never rains but it pours. It is the fact that the river is continuously replenished from the source that keeps the flow going. It is this constant push that allows the river to overcome obstacles either natural or man-made. Even the biggest dam will be breached if the water just keeps on coming. Alternatively, the fiercest river will peter out into a puddle if the source dries up. So before we go on to see which path this particular river takes to the ocean we must be clear that success is only guaranteed as long as the desire to publish remains undiminished.

---

7.   It is not clear whether Rufus was named after one half of the legendary soul
      duo Rufus and Chaka Kahn.

And The Beat Goes On

So now we know the options. Either one or other of the above routes will publish the book, or it will not get published at all. In a nutshell, that is the Age of Aquarius in which we now live. Basically, the only way to plan effectively is to admit that one does not know. Only then can one start to plan for alternative scenarios. It is the prior identification of possible scenarios and the formation of separate plans for the decisions to be made in each of the scenarios that guarantees success in the Age of Aquarius. The swirling vortex that is the external business environment dictates the need for a flexible outlook.

So now that we have identified the available options we can start to move forward along the various paths. The idea is to progress along *each* of the possible routes with the anticipation that *any* of them may turn out to be the most viable option. The goal is to accept that any of the rivers may dry up and in that case the water merely flows into one of the alternative rivers. By the time that all but one of the rivers have been abandoned the main river will have established itself and will be flowing to its maximum force. Once this has occurred, it only takes the persistent precipitation to ensure that the river continues to flow to its ultimate destination.

So What Happened?

Of course in order to complete "*Rock and Roll Economics*", this chapter has been written in advance. However, this is how the story went. The completed manuscript was ready to be sent to David Wilson at Texere. After the London Book Fair in March he was to be sent the next chapter to be completed but at this time he said that he was "too busy" to read odd chapters and that in any case they were moving offices. This sounded like a feeble excuse and was taken with a pinch of salt. He did however say that he would be settled again and ready to read manuscripts by the end of May. It is now early June so it should be timely to contact him. Upon telephoning Texere on the old telephone number a voicemail message was heard. Well, at least they are still around. We need to try again to check whether they did in fact move address. The address on the website has not changed but they never seem to update it so it may still turn out to be a genuine reason. Doubts remain, and it would be a blow to be given such a blatant cold shoulder—but this is the Age of Aquarius and if one avenue closes we merely move on to one of the others. We will try Texere again later.

Alon Shulman had said previously that he would like to see a copy of the finished book. Again this may have been a poor attempt to be polite but it does not matter if it is. His advice was to send it to Texere so he is linked to the success or otherwise of that course of action. If Texere show no interest in the finished product then it must be assumed that Shulman will have no interest in it. It is unlikely that he will read the finished manuscript and change his mind after Texere have rejected it. The only thing that Shulman can do is pitch the book to prospective publishers but as he is not primarily a literary agent he, like Wiley, is only interested if the author is a 'name'.

Texere are still not answering the telephone so they are becoming more and more irrelevant. The options are narrowing and it is looking more and more like the self-publishing route is the best route with the BBC as an optional extra.

The problem with the BBC is that their search for talent will take them all over the United Kingdom and will not end until the end of July.[8] After the search they will choose ten finalists who will be invited to London to make 'tester tapes' for viewing by several television producers. This is the big hurdle. By the time the search has been completed the poor staff in the taxi 'studios' will have seen tens of thousands of potential presenters. The likelihood of getting in the top ten is several

---

8. The two-day visit to the Brighton Festival was in fact the first two days of the three-month long search.

thousand to one. Furthermore, not knowing the outcome for sure until the end of August makes waiting for the outcome a futile exercise. The better option is therefore to pursue the self-publishing route and if the BBC calls then it must be considered a bonus. The publisher concerned is able to publish the book within ninety days, meaning that the finished book could be available by the end of September.

So this was the way it was going to be. The contract was examined briefly. I checked it again before signing the form. A copy of the finished first draft was printed off and made to look as attractive as possible. That was it, then. We will self-publish and be damned. The other rivers had run dry. To heck with Texere and Wiley. To heck with Alon Shulman. To heck with Diane Coyle, but massive respect to David Boyle. It really does seem that if one needs something doing in this world then one has to do it oneself.

The telephone rang and I left my wife to answer it.

"Mick, Mick, it's the BBC on the phone. They want you to come to London. What shall I tell them?"

"Tell them to come to me..."

10
Epilogue

After our team had won a junior school football tournament we were asked to applaud the team that had finished last in the tournament. I asked why we should applaud the losers. After all, we had won the trophy so they should be applauding our team. The teacher said that we should applaud the losers because, unlike my team, the losing team never stood a chance of winning the competition. However they still turned up. He said that if the losing teams had not turned up there would be no tournament, and if there were no tournament our team would not have been able to enjoy the feeling of winning. The moral of the story is that if the winners in the global game of capitalism continue to ridicule the losers, the losers may well stop turning up to the tournament and there will be no more competition to win.

The seeds of the demise of the Anglo-American capitalist system were sown in November 1963 in Dallas, Texas. When the shots rang out it was essentially all over. The new technology in the hands of Abraham Zapruder allowed him to record the whole tragic event. The speed of the camera was known. The shots can be timed from the speed of the footage. The capacity of the rifle was known. In this way the Abraham Zapruder captured a key moment in history.

In the 1990s it was the new technology of the Internet and email that allowed the assassination of the 'goldilocks' economy to be captured for posterity. If the Internet had existed in 1963, the people on the

Grassy Knoll could have sent their stories around the world in a nanosecond. Lee Harvey Oswald might not have been found in the Texas Theatre on West Jefferson. Maybe he would have been found in an Internet café telling the world what really happened. The Anglo-American capitalist system was always built on hypocrisy, but now, if you do not believe that it is all over, then you really have not been paying attention.

History never ends but it is being written every day. Do we want to be ridiculed by our own children? Do we want to be remembered as a race of savages intent on their own destruction and that of the planet on which they reside? Do we want to put individual vanity ahead of social morality? The answers to these questions will be given over time, either in actions or in words. There is no fate but the one we make.

11
Words of Wisdom

"[Chaos theory] is the geometry of the people, in which the *exception* is the rule and the *error* is the correct answer."

"In modern society the most dangerous person is the intelligent, evil person whom society continues to trust despite being continuously let down."

"'Rock and roll economics' is free will within the constraints of a wider society."

"The essence of 'rock and roll economics' is an acceptance of individual freedom, individual choice, and individual dignity."

"In 'rock and roll economics' it is absolutely rational to behave in an irrational and rebellious way."

"It was the struggle with the human condition that gave birth to rock and roll music and it is the struggle with the human and economic condition that has given birth to 'rock and roll economics'."

"Although the financial markets have always been susceptible to herd-like activity, it is the peculiar habits of the sheep that can only describe the actions of the institutional investor."

"Unfortunately the effect [of business schools] has been to produce a generation of managers known more for their meddling mediocrity than their money-making abilities."

"As an old school master once said, *'do whatever you want but don't get caught'*. However it seems that these days it isn't even a crime to get caught."

"The forces of nature are vast and extremely powerful. Nature, and especially human nature will always win. The concept of 'rock and roll economics' is born of this fact."

"Alchemists have always tried to turn lead into gold but modern-day alchemists attempt to *persuade* you that lead *is* gold."

"Economic theory is a necessary simplification for the aid of students of economics and…is a means to control human actions and not merely to reflect it."

"'Rock and roll economics' is an ethos of doing what one wants to do even if it is wrong."

"No government or society that purports to be free can seriously expect to protect citizens from making bad decisions. This is because the ability to make a bad decision is at the heart of personal freedom."

"From over-spending to over-eating, freedom is about getting it wrong occasionally."

12
Bibliography

Roger Bootle, *The Death Of Inflation*, Nicholas Brealey, 1997

David Charters, *Charters on Charting*, Rushmere Wynne, 1995

Edward de Bono, *Tactics*, Fontana/Collins, 1985

Charles D. Ellis, *Winning The Losers Game*, McGraw-Hill, 1998

J.K. Galbraith, *The Great Crash 1929*, Hamish Hamilton, 1955

William R. Gallacher, *Winner Takes All*, Probus Publishing, 1994

Benjamin Graham, *The Intelligent Investor*, Harper Business, 1973

Moira Johnston, *Takeover*, Bantam Press, 1987

Paul Krugman, *Peddling Prosperity*, W.W. Norton, 1995

Michael Lewis, *Liar's Poker*, Hodder & Stoughton, 1989

Janet Lowe, *Warren Buffett Speaks*, J Wiley, 1997

Roger Lowenstein, *When Genius Failed*, Fourth Estate, 2002

Mark H. McCormack, *What They Don't Teach You At Harvard Business School*, Fontana, 1986

George Soros, *Staying Ahead Of The Curve*, J Wiley, 1995

George Soros, *The Alchemy Of Finance*, J Wiley, 1987, 1994

James Wallace & Jim Erickson, *Hard Drive*, J Wiley, 1992

About the Author

Born in Northamptonshire, England, in the summer of 1966, Michael Solomon is not afraid to tell it like it is, and a successful career as a business consultant has enabled him to write a book that tackles head-on the realities of modern business.

0-595-28921-5

www.ingramcontent.com/pod-product-compliance
Lightning Source LLC
Chambersburg PA
CBHW031052180526
45163CB00002BA/794